Quick and easy projects
FOR THE WEEKEND
QUILTER

Quick and easy projects
FOR THE WEEKEND
QUILTER

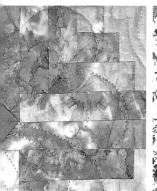

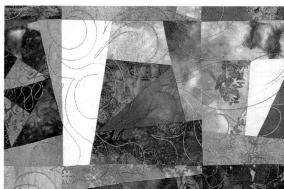

First published in 2002 by
New Holland Publishers (UK) Ltd
London • Cape Town • Sydney • Auckland
www.newhollandpublishers.com

Garfield House, 86-88 Edgware Road, London W2 2EA

80 McKenzie Street, Cape Town 8001, South Africa

Unit 4, 14 Aquatic Drive, Frenchs Forest, NSW 2086,
Australia

218 Lake Road, Northcote, Auckland, New Zealand

2 4 6 8 10 9 7 5 3

ISBN 1 84330 062 1 (PB)

Editor: Rosemary Wilkinson
Design: Frances de Rees
Photographs: Shona Wood
Illustrations: Carrie Hill except pp 72-3 by Coral Mula
Template diagrams: Stephen Dew

Reproduction by Pica Digital PTE Ltd, Singapore
Printed and bound in Malaysia by
Times Offset (M) Sdn Bhd

CONTENTS

Basic quick techniques

Quilting as a technique was probably first encountered by the peoples of Europe when the crusaders returned from their battles. The soldiers of Genghis Khan wore quilted armour. It both protected their bodies and enabled easier movement than the heavy armour used by the Christian armies. Quilted clothing made its way into European culture and was first used mainly as undergarments for warmth and durability.

There is evidence that pieced or patchwork quilts were used as early as the 1600's. Even though patches of fabric or used clothing were pieced together into blankets for warmth, patchwork did not really make much of an impact as an art form until the genteel ladies of the Victorian era began making their intricately pieced and embroidered crazy patch throws or quilt covers.

Patchwork is probably most frequently associated with the pioneering Settlers making a new life in America. Of necessity they used every scrap of fabric available to make quilts to keep their families warm in the harsh winters. It is probable that the pieced "blocks" so associated with American patchwork were first created to enable them to stitch while making the long journeys to find a new home.

During the bicentennial celebrations of the American Independence there was a great resurgence in the craft, which in turn spawned the enormous worldwide quilting industry of today. This industry and the quilters who feed it have created the many and varied tools which make the craft so much easier and faster today. These tools not only enable patchwork to be assembled with speed but also produce a greater accuracy in the cutting and piecing of the patches. The quilts in this book all make use of these tools and techniques.

FABRICS
Fabric selection is always a personal choice. To make the quilts in this book it is not necessary to use the same fabrics that the makers did. In fact, it probably will not be possible to do so as the availability of fabrics is forever changing.

To make a successful quilt there needs to be a difference in tonal values – fabrics that read as light, medium or dark. A selection of fabrics can be all "light" or "dark" but amongst them there should be a difference in value – depth of colour. To help in seeing these values when viewing them, squint your eyes, look through a camera, or the wrong end of binoculars. A variation in the scale of the design – if using a print fabric – can also add interest to a quilt. The addition of plain fabrics or those that read plain, such as tone-on-tone prints, can also enhance the overall appearance of a quilt. There are many beautiful fabrics available today that resemble those with hand-dyed finishes and whose unusual properties can add greatly to the finished effect of your quilt.

Quantities
The quantities given at the beginning of each project have been calculated to allow for a bit extra – just in case! The various pieces/strips cut for each quilt use the rotary cutting method and, unless otherwise stated, are cut from across the width of the fabric. Templates are sometimes used to cut shapes.

A few of the quilts combine cutting on the length of the fabric with cutting across the width. This is to make the most economical use of fabric or to obtain border pieces cut in one piece.

Unless otherwise stated any ¼ yard/ 25 cm requirement is the "long" quarter – the full width of the fabric - and not the "fat" quarter which is a piece 18 x 22 in/ 50 x 56 cm.

Types
100% cotton is probably the easiest to handle but fabric types are very much a personal preference and are, of course, chosen for specific projects. Bed quilts are usually made using 100% cottons but for wall hangings or "art quilts" – anything goes. Two of the makers in this book have also made a feature of flannels and brushed cottons.

Preparation
All fabrics should be washed prior to use in order to wash out any excess dye and to avoid fabrics shrinking at different rates. Wash each fabric separately and rinse – repeatedly if necessary – until the water is clear of any colour run. If washing in a machine, cut a piece of white fabric from a larger piece. Place one piece in with the wash. After the wash, compare the white fabric with its other half. If they are the same, the fabric did not run. If a particular fabric continues to colour the water no matter how many times it is washed/rinsed and you have your heart set on using it, try washing it together with a small piece of each of the fabrics you intend to use with it. If these fabrics retain their original colour i.e. they match the pieces not washed with the offending fabric, you would probably be safe in using it. But if in doubt – don't! Abandon it and choose another.

Once washed and before they are completely dry, iron the fabrics and fold them selvage to selvage – as they were originally on the bolt – in preparation for cutting. Be sure to fold them straight so that the selvages line up evenly.

THREADS
For machine quilting, lightweight or monofilament threads are usual. For quilting by hand, use a thread labelled "quilting thread" which is heavier than normal sewing thread. There are several manufacturers of this thread and it comes in many different colours. Some threads are 100% cotton, others have a polyester core that is wrapped with cotton. You can use a thread either to match or to contrast with the fabric. It is also acceptable to use several colours on the same piece of work.

HOOPS AND FRAMES
The quilt should be held in a hoop or frame for consistency of tension while quilting. There are many types available ranging from hoops, round and oval, to standing frames made of plastic pipes to wooden fixed frames that are in themselves magnificent pieces of furniture.

Hoops are perhaps the easiest for a beginner to start using. The 14 in/35 cm or 16 in/40 cm are best for portability. Many quilters continue to use hoops in preference to standing frames. As with any equipment it all comes down to personal preferences. When the quilt is in the hoop the surface of the quilt should not be taut, as is the case with embroidery. If you place the quilt top with its hoop on a table you should be able to push the fabric in the centre of the hoop with your finger and touch the table beneath. Without this "give" you will not be able to "rock" the needle for the quilting stitch. Whatever you use, never leave the quilt fastened in a hoop. Get into the practice of releasing the outside hoop whenever you leave the quilt – even if only for a few minutes. That few minutes could develop into several days!

EQUIPMENT

The tools of the trade for the modern quilter make life much easier than for those who stitched patchwork in the past. If you are new to patchwork and quilting, the tools available today can be expensive but are well worth the money for the accuracy and speed they afford.

Scissors: These are obviously a necessity. Two pairs are recommended. One pair of good quality scissors should be used for cutting fabric and only fabric. The second pair is for cutting paper, card or template plastic.

Pencils: These will occasionally be required. They need to be sharp at all times to maintain accuracy. The modern "use and throw away" propelling pencils are ideal for this purpose both for drawing around templates and for use in marking quilting designs on quilt tops.

Markers: Quilting designs can either be traced or drawn on the fabric prior to the layering or added after the layering with the aid of stencils or templates. Various marking tools are available: 2H pencils, silver, yellow, white pencils; fade away or washable marking pens. Whatever your choice, test the markers on a scrap of the fabric used in the quilt to ensure that the marks are indeed removable.

Pins: Good quality, clean, rustproof, straight pins are essential when a pin is required to hold the work in place for piecing. Flat-headed flower pins are useful because they don't add bulk.

Safety pins: More and more quilters are beginning to use safety pins to hold the quilt "sandwich" together for the quilting process especially those who prefer to machine quilt or want the speed of not tacking/basting the three layers together.

Needles: For hand quilting use "quilting" or "betweens" needles. Most quilters start with a no. 8 or 9 and progress to a no. 10 or no. 12. The larger the number, the smaller the needle. For machine stitching, the needles numbered 70/10 or 80/12 are both suitable for piecing and quilting. Some makers have needles that are labelled "quilting".

Thimbles: Two thimbles will be required for quilting. One thimble is worn on the hand pushing the needle and one on the hand underneath the quilt "receiving" the needle. There are many types on the market ranging from the usual metal thimbles to those made of plastic to leather sheaths for the finger. There are also little patches that stick to the finger to protect it from the needle pricks. Whatever method is your choice; it is strongly advised that you do use some protection for the fingers on both hands.

ROTARY CUTTING

Rotary cutting has become the most commonly used method to cut fabrics for patchwork today. Special cutters, rulers and mats are needed and with this equipment quilts can be made more accurately and assembled quickly.

Rotary Cutters

There are several different makes available, mainly in three different sizes: small, medium and large. The medium size (45mm) is probably the one most widely used and perhaps the easiest to control. The smallest can be difficult to use with rulers. The largest is very useful when cutting many layers of fabric but can take some practice to use.

Rulers

There are many different rulers available for use with rotary cutters. These are made of acrylic and are sufficiently thick to act as a guide for the rotary blade.

Two sizes of rotary ruler plus a bias square, together with the rotary cutter and self-healing mat; a hoop for quilting and a selection of fat quarters.

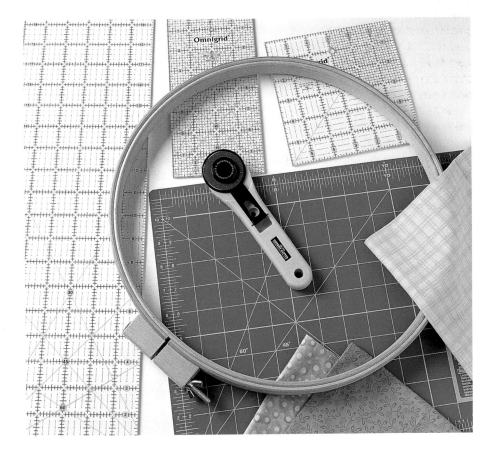

You must use these rulers with the rotary cutter. Do not use metal rulers, as they will severely damage the blades.

Ideally the rulers should have the markings on the underside, laser printed and clear to read. Angle lines are also useful and should be marked in both directions. Different makes of rulers can have the lines printed in different colours. Choose one that you find easy on your eyes. Some makes also have a non-slip surface on the back – a very helpful addition.

To start, the two most useful basic rulers are either a 24 x 6 in/60 x 15 cm or one that is slightly shorter and the small bias square ruler, 6½ in or 15 cm. This ruler is particularly useful for marking squares containing two triangles – the half-square triangle units. There are many other rulers for specific jobs that you can purchase if and when needed.

Self-healing rotary cutting mats

These are an essential companion to the rotary cutter and ruler. Do not attempt to cut on any other surface. The mats come in a number of different sizes and several different colours. The smaller ones are useful to take to classes or workshops but for use at home,

purchase the largest that you feel you can afford and that suits your workstation. There is usually a grid on one side. However, the lines on the mat are not always accurate so get into the habit of using the lines on the ruler. Most rotary cutting tools are available with either imperial or metric measurements.

MEASUREMENTS

The measurements for each project are given in imperial and metric. Use only one set of measurements – do not interchange them because they are not direct equivalents.

Seams

Unless otherwise stated, the seam allowances which will be included in the measurements given are ¼ in for the imperial measurements and 0.75 cm for metric. The metric seam allowance is slightly bigger than the imperial but it is easy to use in conjunction with the various rotary cutting rulers on the market.

If you wish to adapt any of the projects in this book do remember the following when making your calculations:
Imperial: Add the following to the finished size measurements:
Seam allowance: ¼ in
Cutting strips/squares/rectangles: add ½ in
Cutting half-square triangles: add ⅞ in
Cutting quarter-square triangles: add 1¼ in
Metric: Add the following to the finished size measurements:
Seam allowance: 0.75 cm
Cutting strips/squares/rectangles: add 1.5 cm
Cutting half-square triangles: add 2.5 cm
Cutting quarter-square triangles: add 3.5 cm
See diagrams 1 and 2 to see how these measurements are calculated.

diagram 1

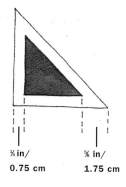

¼ in/ 0.75 cm   ⅞ in/ 1.75 cm

diagram 2

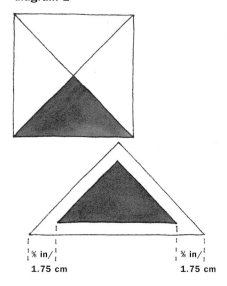

⅞ in/ 1.75 cm   ⅞ in/ 1.75 cm

MAKING THE EDGE STRAIGHT

1 The cut edge of the fabric will probably not be cut straight so place the prepared fabric – folded selvage to selvage – on the cutting mat with the bulk of the fabric on the side that is not your cutting hand. Place the ruler on the fabric aligning the horizontal lines on the ruler with the fold of the fabric and with the selvage.

2 Place your fingers on the ruler to hold it straight and apply pressure. Keep the hand holding the ruler in line with the hand cutting the fabric. Place the cutter on the mat just off the fabric and up against the ruler. Start cutting by running the cutter alongside and right up next to the edge of the ruler (diagram 3).

3 When the cutter becomes level with your extended fingertips, stop cutting but leaving the cutter in position and carefully move the hand holding the ruler further along the ruler to keep the applied pressure in the area where the cutting is taking place. Continue cutting and moving the steadying hand as necessary until you have cut completely across the fabric. As soon as the cut is complete, close the safety shield on the cutter.

4 Open out the narrow strip of fabric just cut off. Check to make sure that a "valley" or a "hill" has not appeared at the point of the fold: it should be perfectly straight. If it is not, the fabric was not folded correctly. Fold the fabric again making sure that this time it is straight. Make another cut to straighten the end and check again.

diagram 3

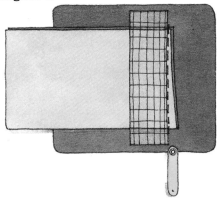

Note:

It is wise when cutting a number of strips – say for a log cabin quilt – to open out a strip occasionally and check that it is still straight at the point of the fold. A slight error on one or two strips is not a disaster but the more strips you cut the greater the error and you can end up with strips that cannot be used.

CUTTING STRIPS

1 Once the end is straight, put the fabric on the cutting mat on the side of your cutting hand. Place the ruler on the mat so that it overlaps the fabric. The cut edge of the fabric should be aligned with the vertical line on the ruler that corresponds to the measurement that you wish to cut and the horizontal lines on the ruler should be aligned with the folded edge and the selvage of the fabric.
2 As before place one hand on the ruler to apply pressure while cutting the fabric with the other hand (diagram 4).

diagram 4

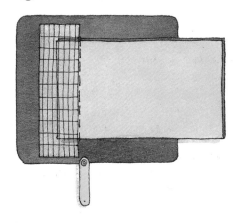

CROSS-CUTTING
Squares
1 First cut a strip to the measurement required.
2 Place the strip just cut on the cutting mat with the longest edge horizontal to you. Straighten off one end as before.
3 Now cut across (cross-cut) the strip using the same measurement used when cutting the strip and ensuring that the horizontal lines of the ruler align with the horizontal edge of the fabric. You have now created squares of the required measurement (diagram 5).

diagram 5

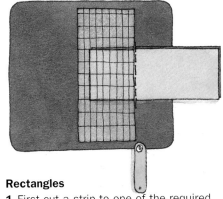

Rectangles
1 First cut a strip to one of the required side measurements for the rectangle.
2 Turn the strip to the horizontal position as for the squares.
3 Cross-cut this strip using the other side measurement required for the rectangle. Again, ensure that the horizontal lines of the ruler align with the horizontal cut edges of the strip.

Wide strips
Placing two rulers side by side can aid the cutting of wider strips. If you don't have two rulers, place the fabric on the cutting mat in the correct position for cutting. Align the cut edge of the fabric with one of the vertical lines running completely across the cutting board and the folded edge with one of the horizontal lines on the mat. If the measurement does not fall on one of the lines on the cutting mat, use the ruler in conjunction with the cutting mat.

Half-square Triangles
1 Cut a strip to the measurement required.
2 Cross-cut the strip into squares using the same cut measurement.

3 Align the 45° angle line on the ruler with the sides of the square and place the edge of the ruler so that it goes diagonally across the square from corner to corner. Cut the square on this diagonal creating two half-square triangles (diagram 6).

diagram 6

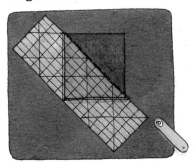

Quarter-square Triangles
1 Cut the fabric into strips of the correct depth.
2 Cut the strips into squares of the correct width.
3 Align the edge of the ruler with diagonally opposite corners and the 45° line with the side of the square, then cut across the diagonal.
4 You can either repeat this procedure on the other diagonal or if you are wary of the fabric slipping now that it is in two pieces, separate the two triangles and cut them individually. Align one of the horizontal lines of the ruler with the long edge of the triangle, the 45° line with the short edge of the triangle and the edge of the ruler placed on the point of the triangle opposite the long edge. Cut this half-square triangle into two quarter-square triangles. Repeat with the remaining half-square triangle (diagram 7).

diagram 7

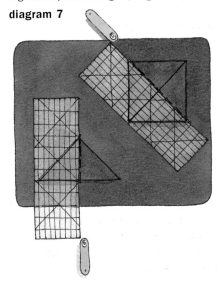

Multi-Strip Units

Cut the required number and size of strips and stitch together as per the instructions for the block/quilt you are making. Press the seams and check that they are pressed flat on the right side of the strip unit with no pleats or folds.

Place the unit right side up in the horizontal position on the cutting mat. This time when cutting to the required measurement there are more reference points to ensure that you are cutting straight. Align the horizontal lines on the ruler with the cut edges of the strips and with the seam lines just created. If after cutting a few cross-cuts the lines on the ruler do not line up with the cut edges as well as the seam lines, re-cut the end to straighten it before cutting any more units (diagram 8).

diagram 8

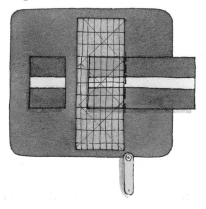

Machine Stitching

As previously mentioned the seam allowances used in this book are the imperial ¼ in or the metric 0.75 cm. To stitch accurately you must be able to use the correct seam allowance and know where this is on your own machine. Many machines today have a "¼ in" or "patchwork" foot available as an extra. There are also various generic foot accessories available which will fit most machines. Don't assume that the foot on your machine is of the correct width. Check first, as follows:

Unthread the machine. Place a piece of paper under the presser foot, so that the righthand edge of the paper aligns with the righthand edge of the presser foot. Stitch a seam line on the paper. A row of holes will appear. Remove the paper from the machine and measure the distance from the holes to the edge of the paper. If it is not the correct width try one of the following methods.

1 If your machine has a number of different needle positions, try moving the needle in the direction required to make the seam allowance accurate. Try the test of stitching a row of holes again. If this does not work, there is another way.

2 Draw a line on the paper to the correct seam allowance, i.e. ¼ in/0.75 cm from the edge of the paper. Place the paper under the presser foot aligning the drawn line with the needle. Lower the presser foot to hold the paper securely and to double check, lower the needle to ensure that it is directly on top of the drawn line.

Now put some masking tape on the bed of the machine so that the lefthand edge of the tape lines up with the righthand edge of the paper. This can also be done with magnetic strips available on the market to be used as seam guides. But do take advice on using these if your machine is computerized or electronic.

When stitching pieces together, line the edge of the fabric up with the righthand edge of the presser foot. Assuming that the foot is of the correct width or that you have moved the needle into a position to create the correct width, this will give you an accurate seam allowance. If you have used tape or the magnetic strip on the bed of your machine, line the righthand edge of the fabric up with the lefthand edge of the tape to give you an accurate seam allowance.

To double check, cut three strips of fabric 1½ in/4 cm wide. Stitch these together. Press the seams away from the centre strip. Measure the centre strip. It should measure exactly 1 in/2.5 cm wide. If not, reposition the needle/tape and try again.

The stitch length used is normally 12 stitches to the inch or 5 stitches to the centimetre. If the pieces being stitched together are to be cross-cut into smaller units, it is probably advisable to slightly shorten the stitch. It is also good practice to start each new project with a new needle in a clean machine – free of fluff around the bobbin housing.

QUICK PIECING

Chain piecing

Chain piecing is a process much used in quick piecing projects. Place the first two pieces or strips in the machine, right sides together, and stitch them together. Just before reaching the end stop stitching and pick up the next two pieces or strips. Place them on the bed of the machine so that they just touch the pieces under the needle. Stitch off one set and onto the next. Repeat this process until all the pairs are stitched. You have created a "chain" of pieced patches/strips (diagram 9). Cut the thread between each unit to separate them. Press the seams according to the instructions given with each project.

diagram 9

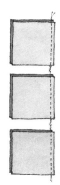

Tip:
To further speed up this process place the two pieces to be stitched together beside the sewing machine. Place one group of patches facing up and one group facing down. Now when you pick up one piece its partner is in the correct position to place on top right sides together.

Pressing

Each individual project will have instructions on the direction in which to press the seam allowances. These have been designed to facilitate easier piecing at junctions and to reduce the bulk so that seam allowances do not lay one on top of the other. Pressing as you complete each stage of the piecing will also improve the accuracy and look of your work. Take care not to distort the patches. Be gentle, not fierce, with the iron.

Two-triangle or Bi-coloured Squares

1 Cut two squares of different coloured fabrics to the correct measurement, i.e. the finished size of square containing the two triangles + ⅞ in/2.5 cm. Place them right sides together aligning all raw edges. On the wrong side of one of the squares draw a line diagonally from one corner to the other.

2 Stitch ¼ in/0.75 cm away on either side of the drawn line.

3 Cut the two halves apart by cutting on the drawn line. You now have two squares each containing two triangles. Press the seams towards the darker of the two fabrics (diagram 10).

diagram 10

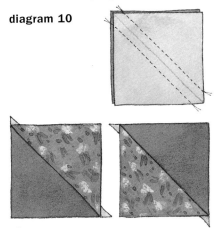

Four-triangle Squares

1 Cut squares to the finished size of a square containing four triangles + 1¼ in/3.5 cm. Follow the stitching, cutting apart and pressing sequence as for two triangles in a square.

2 Place the two squares containing the two triangles right sides together. Ensure that each triangle is not facing a triangle of the same colour. Draw a line diagonally from corner to corner, crossing over the previously stitched seam.

3 Stitch ¼ in/0.75 cm away on either side of this drawn line. Before cutting apart open up each side and check to see that the points match in the centre. Cut apart on the drawn line. You now have two squares each containing four triangles (diagram 11).

diagram 11

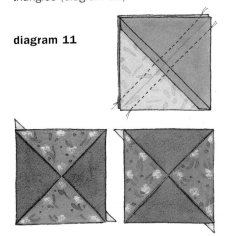

ADDING BORDERS

Abutted Corners

This treatment of the corners on borders for quilts is perhaps the easiest and requires less fabric. The measurements for the borders required for each quilt in the book will be given in the instructions. It is, however, always wise to measure your own work to determine the actual measurement.

1 Measure the quilt through the centre across the width edge to edge. Cut the strips for the top and bottom borders to this length by the width required for the border.

2 Pin the strips to the quilt by pinning first at each end, then in the middle, then evenly spaced along the edge. Pinning in this manner ensures that the quilt "fits" the border. Stitch the border strips into position on the top and bottom edge of the quilt (diagram 12). Press the seams towards the border.

diagram 12

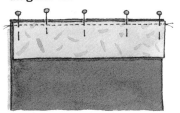

3 Measure the quilt through the centre top to bottom. Cut the side border strips to this measurement.

4 Pin and stitch the borders to the quilt as before (diagram 13). Press the seams towards the border.

diagram 13

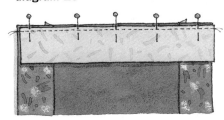

Mitred Corners

This treatment requires a bit more effort but often gives the quilt a more professional finish.

1 Measure the quilt through the centre in both directions. These are the starting measurements for the borders.

2 To these measurements add twice the width of the border, then add seam

allowances of about 2 in/5 cm. Cut strips to the correct measurement for the top, bottom and the sides.

3 On the wrong side of the border fabric, place your rotary cutting ruler with a 45° line on it aligning with one of the long edges of the border. Position the ruler towards one end of the border strip leaving sufficient seam allowance between the edge of the ruler and the end of the strip and draw a line along the edge of the ruler. This will be the mitred corner stitching line (diagram 14).

diagram 14

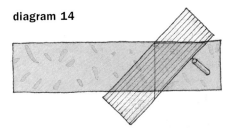

4 Measure ¼ in/0.75 cm up from the edge of the border and make a mark at the point where it crosses the 45° drawn line (diagram 15).

diagram 15

5 From the mark just made measure the length of that border piece – side or top/bottom finished quilt measurement – and make a mark ¼ in/0.75 cm up from the long edge.

6 Align the edge of the ruler with the mark just made, with the ruler pointing out towards the nearest end of the border strip. Align the 45° line on the ruler with the edge of the border strip and draw a line – the stitching line for the mitred corner (diagram 16).

diagram 16

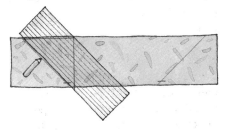

7 Repeat steps 3 to 6 for all four border strips.

8 Place a border strip along the appropriate edge of the quilt. Stick a pin through the mark made ¼ in/0.75 cm from the edge of the border to a corresponding mark made on the quilt top ¼ in/ 0.75 cm from each edge. Pin both ends, the middle and evenly along the edge (diagram 17).

diagram 17

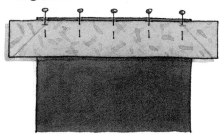

9 Start stitching the border to the quilt at the mark, securing with backstitching and continue to the mark at the other end also securing by backstitching. Open out and press the seam. Stitch on all four borders in this manner.

10 Fold the quilt diagonally, so that two adjacent border strips are right sides together. Align the drawn mitre lines by sticking pins in on the line on the border piece laying on top and ensuring that the pin comes out on the line on the border piece underneath (diagram 18).

diagram 18

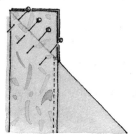

11 Stitch the two border pieces together along the drawn line and up to the point where they meet the quilt. Secure by backstitching. Open out the border and check that the seam just stitched is correct. Trim the excess fabric to the ¼ in/0.75 cm seam allowance. Press the seam open.

QUILTING

The three layers or "sandwich" of the backing/wadding/quilt top are ultimately held together by the quilting. The quilting can either be done by hand or machine.

Layering/Sandwiching

Prior to any quilting, unless you are using a longarm quilting machine (see page 14), the pieced top must be layered with the wadding and the backing. The wadding and the backing should be slightly larger than the quilt top – approximately 2 in/5 cm on all sides.

1 Lay out the backing fabric wrong side uppermost. Ensure that it is stretched out and smooth. Securing the edges with masking tape placed at intervals along the edges can help to hold it in position.

2 Place the wadding on top of the backing fabric. If you need to join two pieces of wadding first, do so by butting the edges and stitching together by hand using a herringbone stitch (diagram 19).

diagram 19

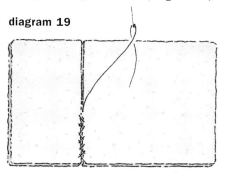

3 Place the pieced top right side up and centred on top of the wadding.

Basting

The three layers now need to be held together for quilting. This can be done by basting by hand or by using safety pins. In either method, start in the centre of the quilt and work out to the edges.

Using a long length of thread start basting in the centre of the quilt top. Only pull about half of the thread through as you start stitching. Once you have reached the edge, go back and thread the other end of the thread and baste to the opposite edge. Repeat this process stitching in a grid over the whole quilt top (diagram 20).

diagram 20

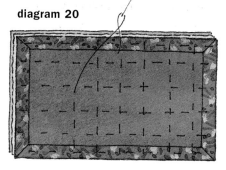

Machine Quilting

In this form of quilting a continuous line of stitching will be visible both on the top and on the back of the quilt. Many consider machine quilting to be the quicker option. If the quilting is mainly functional and not highly decorative, perhaps this is true. However, to machine quilt well – as with any discipline – takes practice.

> **Tip:**
> If basting for machine quilting keep the stitches on the top short so they do not so easily catch on the foot of the machine.
> If using safety pins, these should also be placed at intervals over the quilt top forming a grid with each pin being no further apart than the width of your hand. The pins used should be fine and rustproof like the ones dry cleaners use.

Before commencing work on the quilt, make up a practice sandwich – if possible using the same fabrics and wadding as used in the quilt top. Using the threads that you intend to use on the quilt, have a practice session to determine the effect you want.

Note: For easier handling, roll a large quilt "scroll" fashion to fit within the machine space.

Some machines require a walking foot to stitch the three layers together. These are used with the feed dogs up and, while in use, the machine controls the direction and stitch length. This can restrict you to only straight line quilting, such as "in the ditch" (stitching just beside a seam line on the side without the seam allowances) or very gentle curves. Tight curves and any freehand quilting will be done using a darning foot with the feed dogs down.

When starting and stopping the stitching during machine quilting, either reduce the stitch length to zero or stitch several stitches in one spot. If you do not like the build up of stitches that this method

thumb push the needle into the fabric until it hits the thimble on the finger of the hand underneath the quilt. You will feel the resistance in the sewing hand when they meet.

3 The needle can now be held between the thimble on your sewing hand and the thimble on the finger underneath. Release your thumb and first finger hold on the needle. Place your thumb on the quilt top just in front of the position where the needle will come back up to the top and gently press down on the quilt top (diagram 21).

diagram 21

4 At the same time rock the thread end of the needle back down towards the quilt top and push the needle up from underneath so that the point appears on the top of the quilt. You can either pull the needle through now making only one stitch or rock the needle up to the vertical again, push the needle into the quilt top, then rock the needle back down to the quilt top again placing another stitch on the needle. Repeat until you can no longer rock the needle into a completely upright position. Pull the needle through the quilt (diagram 22).

diagram 22

5 One stitch at a time or several placed on the needle at once – "the rocking stitch" – before pulling the thread

produces, leave long tails on the thread when you start and stop. Later pull these threads through to one side of the quilt, knot them and then thread them into a needle. Push the needle into the fabric and into the wadding but not through to the other side of the quilt and then back out through the fabric again about 1 in/2.5 cm away from where the needle entered the quilt. Cut off the excess thread.

Free Motion Machine Quilting

When machine quilting in a freehand manner, a darning foot is used with the feed dogs down. With this machine set-up, you can move the quilt forwards, backwards and sideways. This is easier on some machines than on others but it takes hours of practice to do it well. Designs to be used for machine quilting should ideally be those that have one continuous line. If using a free form squiggle as a background, be sure to keep the density of stitching the same. Don't get over enthusiastic when you start and make the stitching designs close together only to tire of the process later and begin to space them out.

There are many and varied tools on the market which are designed to help make handling the quilt easier during the machine quilting process.

Hand Quilting

The stitch used for hand quilting is a running stitch. The needle goes into the quilt through to the back and returns to the top of the quilt all in one movement. The aim is to have even stitches. Size of stitches and spaces between the stitches should ideally all be the same.

1 Cut an 18 in/45 cm length of quilting thread and thread the needle. The end just cut is the end to knot. This helps prevent the thread twisting and knotting, as you sew. Start by tying a knot about ½ in/1.25 cm from the end of the thread. Push the needle into the fabric and into the wadding but not through to the back about 1 in/2.5 cm away from where you want to start stitching. Bring the needle up through the fabric at the point where you will begin stitching. Gently pull on the thread to "pop" the knot through into the wadding.

2 To make a perfect quilting stitch the needle needs to enter the fabric perpendicular to the quilt top. Holding the needle between your first finger and

through, are both acceptable. When the stitching is complete, tie a knot in the thread close to the quilt surface. Push the needle into the quilt top and the wadding but not through to the back of the quilt. Bring the needle up again about 1 in/2.5 cm away and gently tug on the thread to "pop" the knot through the fabric and into the wadding. Cut the thread.

Big Stitch

There is another form of hand quilting popular today, known as the "Big Stitch", which can speed up the process of quilting by hand and adds yet another design element. Big Stitch uses coton perlé no. 8 as the thread and a larger needle with a bigger eye. The stitches are also larger and simplicity is required for the quilting designs used. It can be very effective but is not necessarily suited to all quilts. Apart from simple designs any outline quilting is normally ½ in/1.25 cm from the seam lines rather than the ¼ in/0.75 cm used with traditional hand quilting. The quilting stitch for the "Big Stitch" is also a running stitch.

Longarm Quilting Machines

Since the advent of longarm quilting machines it is possible to have quilt tops professionally quilted. You can choose from a huge library of quilting designs. There is also the option to have edge-to-edge quilting; all-over quilting of one design over the entire quilt, or a combination of patterns to complement each other, e.g. medallions, feathers, cables and cross-hatching. Alternatively, you can specify your own freehand style.

The quilt top, wadding and backing are mounted onto separate rollers which are part of the frame of the machine. This means that the three layers of the quilt need not be tacked together in the conventional way.

The machine is hand operated and takes considerable skill to operate successfully. Most of the quilters who offer these services advertise in patchwork magazines and will provide you with an explanatory brochure.

BINDING

Once the quilting is completed the quilt is usually finished off with a binding to enclose the raw edges. This binding can

be cut on the straight or on the bias. Either way the binding is usually best done with a double fold. If cut straight, cut the strips then join together to form one continuous strip. If bias cut, join the strips with a diagonal seam (diagram 23).

diagram 23

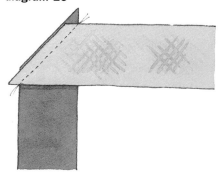

To make continuous bias binding

1 Cut a square of fabric and mark the edges, A, B, C and D. Cut in half by cutting on the diagonal. With right sides together place side A on top of side B and stitch with the usual ¼ in/0.75 cm seam allowance (diagram 24).

diagram 24

2 Open out the unit and press the seam open. On the wrong side draw lines to mark the width of the bias strips you require (diagram 25).

diagram 25

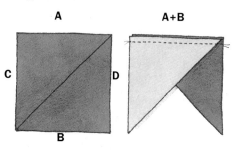

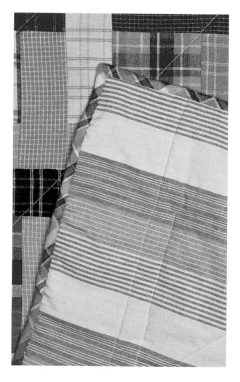

3 With right sides together, join side C to side D, but instead of matching the drawn lines, offset them by one row. Pin the edges to ensure that the lines match. Stitch, then press the seam open.
4 Now using scissors cut along the drawn line following it around the tube you have just created (diagram 26).

diagram 26

Double-fold binding

The width of the bias strips should be cut to the following measurement: finished binding width x four + the seam allowance x two. Example:
A finished binding width of ½ in would be cut as 2½ in: (½ in x 4) + (¼ in x 2) = 2½ in
or 1.25 cm would be cut 6.5 cm:
(1.25 cm x 4) + (0.75 cm x 2) = 6.5 cm

1 Fold the binding in half lengthwise with wrong sides together and lightly press.
2 Place the binding's raw edges to the raw edge of the quilt – somewhere along one side, not at a corner. Commence

stitching about 1 in/2.5 cm from the end of the binding and using ¼ in/0.75 cm seam allowance stitch the binding to the quilt through all layers of the "sandwich" stopping ¼ in/0.75 cm from the end. At this point backstitch to secure, then break off the threads. Remove the quilt from the sewing machine.

3 Place the quilt on a flat surface with the binding just stitched at the top edge, fold the binding strip up and away from the quilt to "twelve o'clock", creating a 45° fold at the corner (diagram 27).

diagram 27

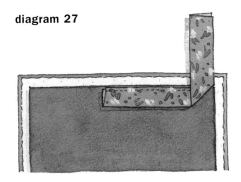

4 Fold the binding back down to "six o'clock" aligning the raw edge of the binding to the raw edge of the quilt. The fold created on the binding at the top should be the same distance away from the seam as the width of the finished binding. i.e. ½ in/1.25 cm from seam line to fold (diagram 28).

diagram 28

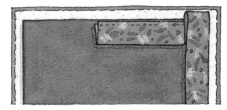

5 Start stitching the binding to the quilt top at the same point the previous stitching stopped, ¼ in/0.75 cm from the edge of the quilt top. Secure with backstitching, then continue to the next corner. Repeat the process at each corner.
6 Stop about 2 in/5 cm from where you started. Open out the fold on both ends of the binding, then seam the two ends together. Trim away the excess, refold and finish applying the binding to the quilt.
7 Trim the excess wadding and backing fabric so that the distance from the stitching line equals or is slightly wider than that of the finished binding. Fold

the binding over onto the back and hand stitch the folded edge of the binding to the quilt along the row of machine stitching just created. A mitre will appear at the corners on the front and on the back of the binding. Slipstitch these in place to secure (diagram 29).

diagram 29

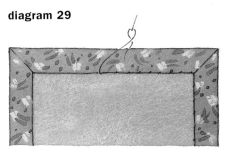

Hanging Sleeve

If your quilt is a wall hanging or is to be exhibited it will need a hanging sleeve. A sleeve can be added after the quilt is completely finished but a more secure and permanent sleeve can be added at the time of adding the binding. Stitch the binding to the front of the quilt and before folding it over onto the back add the sleeve.

1 Cut a piece of fabric, preferably matching the backing, to measure 10 in/25 cm by the width of the quilt. Make a 1 in/2.5 cm hem on both the short ends.
2 Fold the fabric in half along the length with wrong sides together. Centre this on the back of the quilt aligning the raw edges of the sleeve with the raw edges of the quilt. Secure with pins (diagram 30).

diagram 30

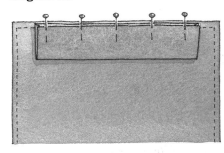

3 Turn the quilt over so the front is uppermost. Taking care to remove the pins as you approach them, stitch the sleeve to the quilt along the row of stitching made when applying the binding.
4 Finish hand stitching on the binding.
5 Lay the quilt on a flat surface with the back uppermost. Gently roll the top layer of the tube up to the top edge of the binding so it forms a fold along this

edge. Secure with pins. Now smooth out the rest of the sleeve tube until it rests evenly on the back of the quilt (diagram 31).

diagram 31

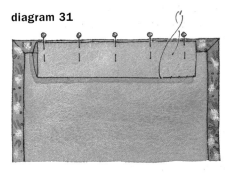

6 Stitch the sleeve to the back of the quilt along the fold at the bottom of the sleeve and at each end so that when a rod is inserted it will not actually touch the back of the quilt only the sleeve fabric. Take care that your stitches only go into the back and wadding of the quilt and are not visible on the front. Remove the pins. The sleeve is now stitched to the quilt and has a slight bulge in it. This bulge will allow room for a rod to go through the sleeve without distorting the quilt when it is hung.

LABELLING

Your quilt should be signed, dated and placed. This information provides a record for your own information as well as for those in the future. A quilt that has this information on it is given more respect than one that does not.

This information can be incorporated on the quilt front or on a label on the back. A label can be very simple with the information written on with a permanent pen or made very elaborate with pieced, embroidered or fabric painting. There are books available on fancy labels and how to make them, with artwork one can copy or adapt. Another way of making an individual label is with the help of today's modern technology, the computer and printer. There are also various supplies available enabling one to print on fabric so that it remains permanent. Whatever method you choose for your quilt – do label it!

COUNTRY WISDOM

Gill Turley

Folklore and country sayings are the theme for this chapter. For some of the quilts the sayings are linked to the names of traditional blocks, for others they have influenced the choice of fabrics and colours in the design.

Steeped in tradition, these words of wisdom are little observations on the weather or on behaviour or just on home comforts, which are still relevant today. They make a good match with classic quilting patterns which are brought up-to-date with contemporary fabrics. Quilters also like to pass on hints and tips from their experience, so I hope the added notes alongside the instructions will assist readers with their quiltmaking.

Most of the quilts are small and therefore quick to produce but they could easily be extended to become larger projects by making extra blocks.

Rain Before Seven, Fine Before Eleven!

A saying which can often prove to be very true! So when the sun comes out take this tablecloth outside and have lunch in the garden. If the saying is proved wrong and the rain does not stop, then use the tablecloth indoors and dream of sunny days!

This simple repeated block pattern is easy to make and a good way of showing off those vibrant, provençal prints. Since the fabric is thick and the intention is to use this cover as a tablecloth, I haven't used any wadding, however it would also make a cheerful cover for a single bed and could be wadded and quilted or tied if desired. Alternatively, it could be made in lightweight wools and used as a throw on a sofa.

MATERIALS

All fabrics are 60 in/152 cm wide

Large print for big squares: red, 24 in/60 cm; blue, 24 in/60 cm
Small print for small squares and rectangle pieces: yellow, 12 in/30 cm; light blue, 12 in/30 cm; dark blue, 16 in/40 cm; bright red, 16 in/40 cm;
Backing fabric: 67 in/170 cm (same amount required for wadding if used)
Cotton à broder in red for tying (optional)

Quilt size: 62 x 50½ in/158 x 128 cm

Quilt assembly diagram

Note:
These small provençal prints are mostly "directional" prints and can look strange if the patterns do not all fall in the same direction. If you follow the cutting plans carefully these prints can easily be accommodated. These diagrams would also help if you are using striped fabrics.

ALTERNATIVE COLOURWAYS

*Four collages of different colourways for the basic block design show how much fabric
choice can affect the mood of the quilt. The top two show summery alternatives; the violets,
bottom left, produce a feminine touch and the patterned reds and browns, bottom right,
give a cosy, country effect.*

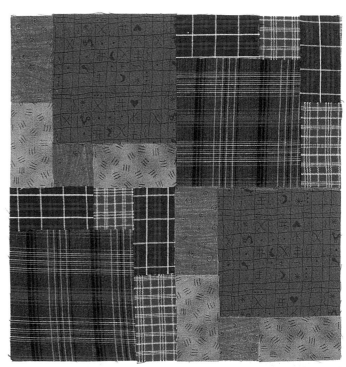

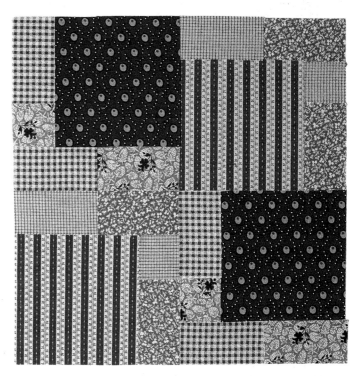

CUTTING

Refer to diagrams, measure twice, cut once!

- **Large prints**, cut 10 red and 10 blue squares, 9½ x 9½ in/25.5 x 25.5 cm
- **Small provençal prints: yellow and light blue only** (diagram 1), cutting across the width of the fabric, cut 3 strips, each 3½ in/8 cm wide. Save one of each colour to make the top and bottom borders, then cut the remaining strips into rectangles 6½ x 3½ in/17.5 x 8 cm as follows:
10 yellow and 10 light blue horizontal rectangles (with the long edge of the rectangle horizontal to the pattern). From the remaining fabric cut 10 blue and 10 yellow squares 3½ x 3½ in/8 x 8 cm.

diagram 1

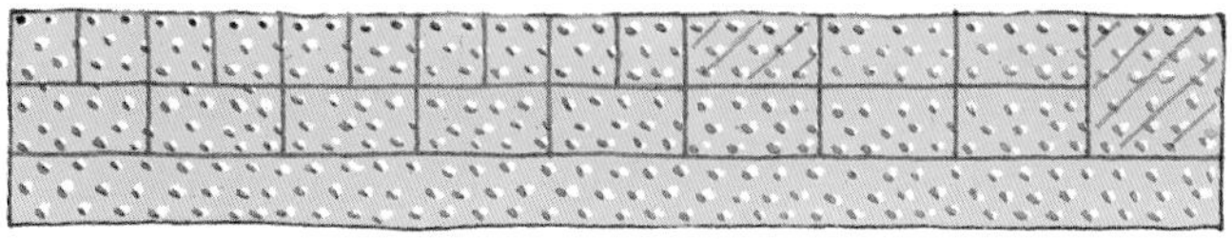

- **Small provençal prints: dark blue and bright red only** (diagram 2), cutting across the width of the fabric, cut one strip 6½ in/16.5 cm wide and cut from this 10 vertical rectangles (with the long edge of the rectangle vertical to the printed pattern). Cut one more long strip 3½ in/8 cm wide from each of the remaining pieces of dark blue and bright red fabrics, from these strips and the leftover fabric from the first strips cut 10 rectangles with the long edge of the rectangle horizontal to the pattern.

diagram 2

![diagram 2]

STITCHING

Note:
All seams allowances are ¼ in/0.75 cm. All seams should be pressed open to accommodate the thickness of the fabric. There are two blocks A and B (diagrams 3 and 4). The diagrams will help you position the pieces so that the small prints all run in the same direction.

Block A (diagram 3)

1 Stitch a small yellow square to the base of a bright red vertical rectangle.

2 Stitch this unit to the righthand edge of the large blue square. (Note, the yellow square should now be at the bottom righthand corner of the large blue square.)

3 Stitch a yellow horizontal rectangle to a bright red one along one short edge, so that the yellow is on the left and the red is on the right. Stitch this unit to the base of the large square unit.

4 Repeat steps 1 to 3 for the other nine A blocks.

diagram 3

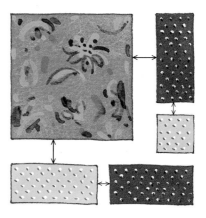

Block B (diagram 4)

5 Stitch a small light blue square to the top of a dark blue vertical rectangle.

6 Stitch this unit to the lefthand edge of the large red square. (Note, the small blue square will now be at the top lefthand corner of the large square.)

7 Stitch a dark blue horizontal rectangle to a light blue one along one short edge, so that the dark blue is on the left and the light blue on the right. Stitch this unit to the top of the large red square.

diagram 4

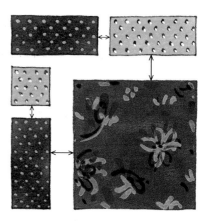

8 Repeat steps 5 to 7 for the other nine B blocks.

9 Stitch the completed blocks into rows as follows:
BABA
ABAB
BABA
ABAB
BABA

10 Press all seams open, then stitch the rows together, making sure that where seams meet, they match exactly.

11 Lay out the backing fabric on a flat surface, wrong side up, making sure that there are no folds or creases. Place the pieced top over the backing, right side up.

12 Cut off the excess fabric along the length of the backing fabric and keep it for the two side borders. These should measure 3½ in/8 cm wide x length of pieced top.

13 Tack the top and bottom layers together in a grid, keeping them very flat. You may like to use a fabric spray glue to help secure the two layers.

ADDING THE BORDERS

> **Note:**
> Take care that the directional print on the border follows the same direction as the prints on the front of the cloth. Change your bobbin and top threads with each border to match the different border colours. You will see that I have chosen to put the yellow border along the top edge of the cloth and the blue at the bottom, this way neither border touches another piece of the same coloured fabric.

1 Press the two side borders in half lengthwise to make a fold, open again, then pin the borders to the side edges of the cloth.

2 Working from the back, stitch through both the front and back of the tablecloth and one layer of border fabric (diagram 5). Press the seam towards the border.

diagram 5

3 Bring the border to the front of the cloth, folding on the pressed line and turn under ¼ in/0.75 cm on the long edges. Pin and tack, then top stitch in place, selecting the thread colour to match the border.

4 Measure the pieced top from side to side including the added borders and add ½ in/1.5 cm total seam allowance. Trim the two remaining border strips, light blue and yellow, to this measurement.

5 Press both borders in half lengthwise, wrong sides together. Turn under the seam allowance on each short end of the borders. Pin and tack the borders to the top and bottom edges of the tablecloth, then stitch in place as before (diagram 6). Finish by slip stitching the corners.

diagram 6

FINISHING

1 To make sure that the two layers do not move when the cloth is laundered, I have tied the tablecloth placing a tie in each corner of the large squares.

2 Alternatively, machine stitch around the large squares, stitching "in the ditch" and using matching threads.

Enough Blue in the Sky

Enough blue in the sky to make a pair of sailor's trousers: a delightful saying meaning that if there is enough blue sky showing before midday, then the weather will probably stay fine.

Using blue and white to echo this theme I have made a little cot quilt. The method used produces leftover two triangle squares which could be used to make a cradle quilt or a cushion (as shown in the photograph on the cover). This is definitely a case of "waste not, want not" or "two for the price of one". This block pattern is sometimes known as "Indian Hatchet" or if the centre section is made from a plain fabric and signed it also goes by the name of "signature block".

MATERIALS

All fabrics used in the quilt top are 45 in/115 cm wide, 100% cotton

Plain blue: 45 in/115 cm
Large check: 67 in/170 cm
Wadding: cotton or fine polyester, 45 x 38 in/115 x 97 cm (for cradle quilt: 29½ x 26 in/74.5 x 65.5 cm)
Backing: same amount as for the wadding.
Binding (small check): 26 x 26 in/66 x 66 cm (for cradle quilt: 20½ x 20½ in/52 x 52 cm)
Machine quilting threads: to match the fabric colours on front and back of quilt
Tracing paper: one A4 sheet
Thin card: one A4 sheet
Chalk marker

Quilt size: 42½ x 35½ in/108 x 90 cm

Quilt assembly diagram

CUTTING

● **Plain blue**, cut 40 squares, 6 x 6 in/15 x 15 cm. Save the spare fabric for the corner squares on the borders, cut these later.

● **Large check**, cutting across the width of the fabric, cut 20 squares, 8 x 8 in/20 x 20 cm. Save the spare fabric for borders, cut these later.

STITCHING

1 Fold each blue square in half on the diagonal and press. On wrong side of fabric draw a line ½ in/1.5 cm to the right of the pressed line (diagram 1).

diagram 1

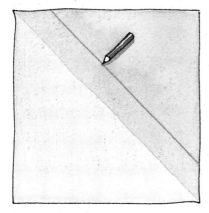

2 Take one blue square and place it, right sides together, in the top righthand corner of a large check square, making sure that edges match exactly. Stitch on the pressed line and the drawn line (diagram 2).

diagram 2

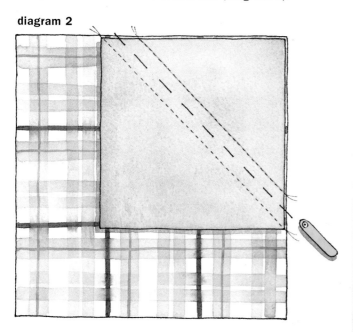

3 Cut midway between the lines of stitching, cutting through both layers of fabric. Press the seam towards the blue corner.

4 Repeat steps 2 and 3, but this time place the blue square in the bottom lefthand corner, stitch and trim as before. Press the seam towards the blue corner.

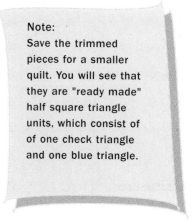

Note:
Save the trimmed pieces for a smaller quilt. You will see that they are "ready made" half square triangle units, which consist of of one check triangle and one blue triangle.

5 Continue in the same way until all twenty blocks have been completed.

6 Following the quilt assembly diagram on page 22, stitch the blocks together making five rows of four blocks. Press the seams of each row in alternate directions.

7 Stitch the rows together and press.

ADDING THE BORDERS

1 Measure the pieced top from centre top to centre bottom and cut two side borders from the remaining check to this measurement and 3¾ in/9.5 cm wide.

2 Measure the pieced top from centre side to centre side and cut two borders from the check to this measurement, 3¾ in/9.5 cm wide, for the top and bottom borders.

3 Stitch the side borders to the side edges of the quilt and press the seams towards the borders.

4 From the remaining blue fabric cut four squares for the corners, 3¾ x 3¾ in/9.5 x 9.5 cm.

5 Join the blue squares to each end of the top and bottom borders. This time press the seams towards the check fabric.

6 Stitch the borders to the top and bottom of quilt and press the seams towards the border.

FINISHING

1 Layer the quilt top, wadding and backing and tack or pin the layers together ready for machine quilting.

2 Begin by outline stitching inside the centre sections of the blocks, using the width from the needle to the edge of the machine foot as a width guide. This will be ¼ in/0.75 cm or wider, it does not matter as long as the measurement remains consistent. The thread ends should be hidden and are best run in afterwards, by hand.

3 Trace the template below onto the tracing paper, cut out and stick the tracing paper to the thin card. Cut the card to shape along the solid lines.

4 Place the template on a blue triangle and draw round it with a chalk marker, following the quilting lines. Quilt the blue triangles, starting the zig-zag at the top of the tallest line and stitching down and up the zig-zags. When you come to the end of the shortest zig-zag, stitch "in the ditch" until you are in position to begin stitching on the shortest line of the next triangle. You will see that it is not necessary to cut the thread before commencing the stitching on the next triangle (diagram 3).

diagram 3

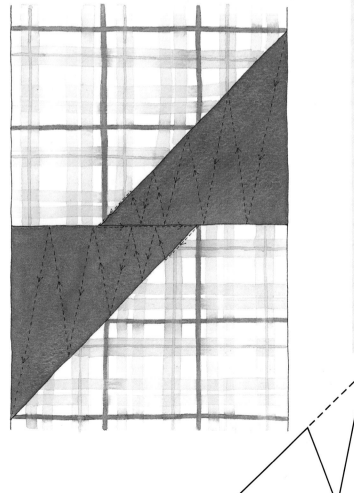

5 Machine quilt the borders in straight lines, using your sewing machine seam guide to keep the lines straight.

6 Make the double bias binding 2 in/5 cm wide using the continuous strip method. Use to bind the edges with a double-fold binding, mitred at the corners.

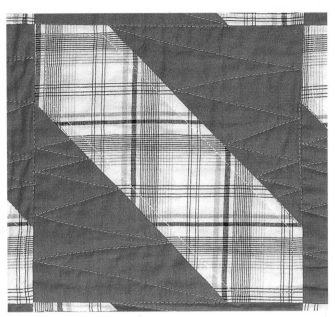

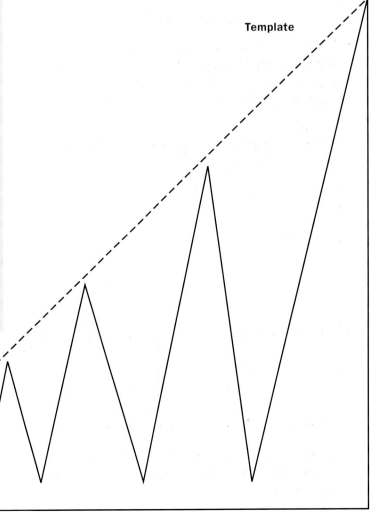

Template

North, South, East, West, Home is the Best

The design for this lap quilt is based on the "windblown square" block. The combination of the green and blue Liberty prints and the white-on-white background fabric produces a very crisp look. The white infill blocks make the pattern float and add movement to the design.

At first glance the blocks may appear more complicated than they actually are; take a closer look and you will see that they are composed of a four patch design. The patterns are created from half square triangle units which are pieced using the grid method.

MATERIALS

All fabrics used in the quilt top are 45 in/115 cm wide, 100% cotton, with non-directional print

Blue small floral print: 12 in/30 cm
Green small floral print: 12 in/30 cm plus 18 x 18 in/50 x 50 cm for binding
White-on-white floral print: 50 in/130 cm plus 39 x 39 in/100 x 100 cm for backing
Wadding: 39 x 39 in/100 x 100 cm
Machine quilting thread: white

Quilt size: approximately 35 x 35 in/90 x 90 cm

Quilt assembly diagram

CUTTING

- **Blue and green small floral prints,** cut 2 squares 12 x 12 in (32 x 32 cm) and 1 square 6 x 6 in/ 16 x 16 cm from each.
- **White-on-white floral print,** cut 4 squares 12 x 12 in/32 x 32 cm and 2 squares 6 x 6 in/16 x 16 cm; cut 4 squares 8½ x 8½ in/21.5 x 21.5 cm and keep these for the plain blocks; cut 2 squares 8½ x 8½ in/21.5 x 21.5 cm and cut these once on the diagonal, keep these for the corner triangles; cut 2 squares 9¼ x 9¼ in/23.5 x 23.5 cm and cut these twice on the diagonal, keep these for the side edge triangles.

STITCHING

1 Place one white 12 in/32 cm square with one blue square, right sides together with the white fabric on top. Repeat with a pair of green and white squares. Repeat to make two more pairs with the blue, green and white fabrics. Steam-press to help prevent fabrics from slipping.

2 Using a sharp pencil, mark a 3 in/8 cm grid on each pair on the white fabric. Next mark diagonal lines through the grids in one direction only (diagram 1).

diagram 1

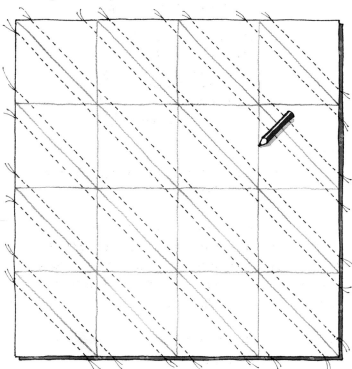

3 Stitch on both sides of the diagonal lines using ¼ in/0.75 cm seam allowance.

4 When all the stitching is complete cut through all grid lines and all diagonal lines. Each grid square will yield two half square triangle units (diagram 2). Ease apart gently at the points and press seams.

diagram 2

5 Place one white 6 in/16 cm square with one blue square, right sides together with the white fabric on top. Repeat with a pair of green and white squares. Steam-press.

6 Mark with a 3 in/8 cm grid, stitch and cut as in steps 2 to 4.

7 Press the units, pressing the seams together towards the darker triangle. Trim all units to an accurate 2½ x 2½ in/6.5 x 6.5 cm.

> Note:
> The grid is intentionally generous allowing for any minor discrepancies during the first stage.

8 Stack the trimmed units in the block arrangement (diagram 3).

diagram 3

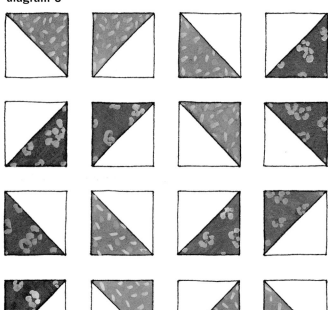

9 Taking care not to change the arrangement, chain stitch the first two units in row 1 to those in row 2 without cutting the thread between the units (diagram 4).

diagram 4

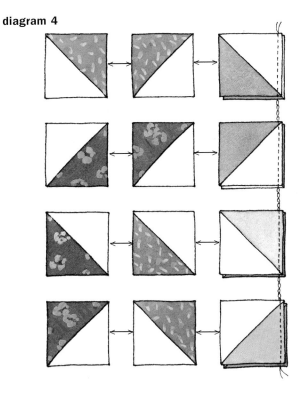

10 Do the same with rows 3 and 4. Next join row 2 to row 3 so that all vertical seams are joined.

11 With the units still attached to each other, press the seams open.

12 Join the rows horizontally taking great care to match points. To do this, begin by pinning on each side of the joins where the points meet and stitch just across the join. Before stitching the whole row from end to end check that all points meet accurately.

13 When all nine pieced blocks are complete, press all the seams open.

14 Following the quilt assembly diagram on page 26, lay out the blocks with the plain infill squares and the side and corner triangles.

15 Stitch the blocks into diagonal rows (diagram 5).

diagram 5

16 Stitch the diagonal rows together, putting on the corner triangles last. Press all the seams open.

> Note:
> The side and corner triangles will overhang a little but can be carefully trimmed if liked using a long ruler and making use of the 45 degree markings.

FINISHING

1 Layer the backing fabric, wadding and top and baste ready for machine quilting.

2 Using white thread, quilt with an outline stitch ¼ in/0.75 cm inside the middle square of the pieced block. On the infill white squares and triangles, machine quilt ¼ in/0.75 cm in from the seam line, then stitch a second line inside to echo the first.

3 Make the double bias binding 2 in/5 cm wide from the green 18 in/50 cm square, using the continuous strip method. Use to bind the edges with a double fold binding, mitred at the corners.

Something Old, Something New

Something old, something new, something borrowed, something blue: a traditional saying, advising that on her wedding day every bride should wear one of each of the above items to bring her luck. Blue is said to be the colour of heaven and shows constancy. There are many customs and superstitions linked to the marriage ceremony: green "the fairies' colour" is considered to be unlucky by some, while white indicates purity and remains popular. I wanted to make a quilt that had an old look and chose this simple pattern using scraps of antique fabrics purchased in the U.S.A. This quilt provides an excellent way of using scraps from your fabric stash, perhaps incorporating those which have special memories.

MATERIALS

Scraps of assorted cotton fabrics: 143 squares 3 x 3 in/8 cm x 8 cm. Choose light, medium and dark tones from within your chosen colour range, e.g. blue, grey, white; but also include a few that will add an element of surprise, such as the reds, pinks and browns.

Or purchased fabric: If you are buying fabric, you will need the following amounts of 45 in/115 cm wide fabric:
bright colour - 8 in/20 cm
dark colour - 12 in/30 cm
light colour - 8 in/20 cm
medium colour - 16 in/40 cm

Border and binding : 52 in total = 30 x 44 in for borders and 22 in square for binding/130 cm total = 75 x 115 cm for borders and 55 cm square for binding

Backing: 44 x 49 in/112 x 125 cm

Wadding: thin cotton, 44 x 49 in/112 x 125 cm

Quilt size: 40½ x 45½ in/103 x 116 cm

Quilt assembly diagram

> **Note:**
> When working with scrap fabric try to use materials of similar weight. If you use old fabric in a quilt, do check carefully to make sure that it has no worn or thin areas. To prevent shrinkage, wash the fabric before use and check that the colours are fast. This also applies to new fabric.

CUTTING

> Note:
> Time can be saved by cutting several layers of fabric at a time, although this is not quite so easy to manage when using scrap fabrics of different dimensions. You may like to cut a few extra squares so that you have more choice when planning your arrangement.

● **Assorted scrap fabrics**, cut a total of 143 squares each 3 x 3 in/8 x 8 cm from bright, dark, light and medium fabrics.

STITCHING

1 Following the quilt assembly diagram on page 30, arrange and pin the squares on a flat surface or design wall if you have one, in thirteen rows of eleven squares. Stand back and look through a spy glass or a reducing glass to get a better idea of the the overall design. I have arranged my design to form diagonal stripes using the majority of the medium and dark blue squares, with just the occasional red square put in for impact. The dark, diagonal rows are spaced with rows made from the lighter fabrics. Don't worry if your design has one or two "rogue squares", for example, a light square where a dark should should be: these will help provide an element of surprise and add to the "antique" look.

2 Stitch the squares into rows. Press the seams in alternate directions.

3 Stitch row 1 to row 2 and continue until all thirteen rows have been joined to form the centre section of the quilt (diagram 1).

diagram 1

ADDING THE BORDERS

1 Measure the pieced top from centre top to centre bottom and cut two borders to this measurement, each 6½ in/16.5 cm wide. Stitch these to the long sides of the patchwork and press the seams towards the borders.

2 Measure the pieced top from the centre of the left-hand edge to the centre of the righthand edge, including the borders just stitched. Use this measurement to cut two borders, each 6½ in/16.5 cm wide. Stitch these to the top and bottom edges of the quilt. Press the seams towards the borders.

FINISHING

1 Layer the backing, wadding and top and baste the layers ready for quilting.

2 This quilt has been hand quilted but machine quilting or tying would be quicker. Use masking tape to mark guidelines for the diagonal quilting and stitch with regular quilting thread and traditional, small running stitch.

3 Make the double bias binding 2 in/5 cm wide from the 22 x 22 in/55 x 55 cm square, using the continuous strip method. Use to bind the edges with a double-fold binding, mitred at the corners.

While the Cat's Away, the Mice Will Play

The "cat and mouse" patchwork block has many variations, I have used a very simple version for this design. Drafting the design on paper, I repeated the block four times, then decided to replace some of the triangles that would normally fall on the edges of the blocks, with squares. This makes better use of the large print fabric and eliminates some of the seams which would have broken up the centre of the design. The design is enclosed with a border of triangles. The finished arrangement reminds me of an old-fashioned board game.

MATERIALS

All fabrics used in the quilt top are 45 in/115 cm wide, 100% cotton

Large print: 24 in/60 cm
Rust, tiny check: 6 in/15 cm
Stripe: 12 in/30 cm
All-over print (a): 24 in/60 cm for pieced triangle units and outer border triangles, see also note for backing
All-over print (b): 6 in/15 cm for pieced triangle units
All-over print (c): 24 in/60 cm for inner border triangles
Wadding: lightweight, 44 x 44 in/112 x 112 cm
Backing: (Note: this can be of the same fabric as the outer border triangles) 44 x 44 in/112 x 112 cm

Quilt size: 39½ x 39½ in/101 x 101 cm

Quilt assembly diagram

CUTTING

● **Large print**, cut 4 squares, 8⅞ x 8⅞ in/22.5 x 22.5 cm, then cut these once on the diagonal to make 8 large triangles;
cut 4 squares 8½ x 8½ in/21.5 x 21.5 cm;
cut 9 squares 4½ x 4½ in/11.5 x 11.5 cm.
● **Rust, tiny check**, cut 8 squares, 4½ x 4½ in/11.5 x 11.5 cm.
● **Stripe**, cut 12 squares, 4½ x 4½ in/11.5 x 11.5 cm.
● **All-over prints (a) and (b)**, cut 8 squares, 5½ x 5½ in/ 14 x 14 cm, from each.
● **All-over print (a)**, cut strips 7 in/18 cm wide on the straight grain of the fabric, then placing the ruler at 45 degrees to the long edges of the fabric, cut 12 squares, each 4⅞ x 4⅞ in/12.5 x 12.5 cm (diagram 1). Cut these squares in half once on the diagonal to make 24 triangles for the outer border triangles. In this way the short edges fall on the bias grain of the fabric and the long edges on the straight grain of the fabric, which will make the border edges more stable;

diagram 1

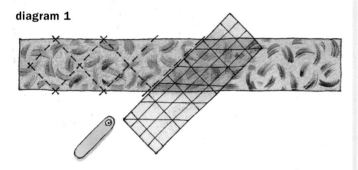

cut 2 squares, 4½ x 4½ in/11.5 x 11.5 cm on the straight grain of the fabric, then cut each square once on the diagonal to make the four corner triangles. Here the short edges of the triangles will fall on the straight grain.

● **All-over print (c)**, cut strips 7 in/18 cm wide on the straight grain of the fabric, then cut 8 squares as before and cut these to make 16 triangles for the inner border triangles.

STITCHING

1 To make the quarter square units, take the eight 5½ in/14 cm squares cut from all-over prints (a) and (b) and pair (a) and (b) squares, right sides together.

2 On the upper, wrong side of each pair of squares draw a diagonal line and stitch ¼ in/0.75 cm away on both sides of the drawn line. Cut on the diagonal lines, open out and press seams together, towards the darker fabric. You will now have 16 two-triangle squares (diagram 2).

diagram 2

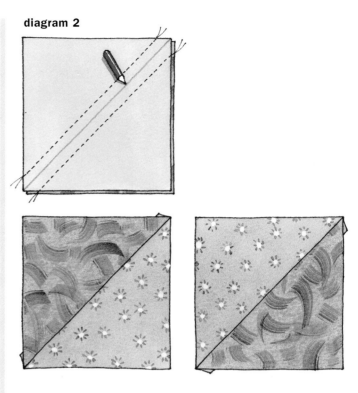

3 Place the units in pairs right sides together, so that the light triangle is on the dark triangle and the centre seams butt together. As before mark diagonal lines, this time from unstitched corner to unstitched corner. Stitch and cut as before. Open out and press the seams. You will now have 16 four-triangle squares (diagram 3).

diagram 3

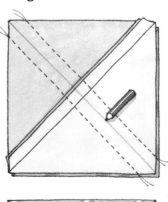

4 The original squares were cut with a generous allowance for piecing. The units can now be trimmed, so that each measures 4½ x 4½ in/11.5 x 11.5 cm.

5 Following diagram 4 and working in rows from the centre out, begin by joining the units for the centre (row 1) but do not add the corner triangles.

diagram 4

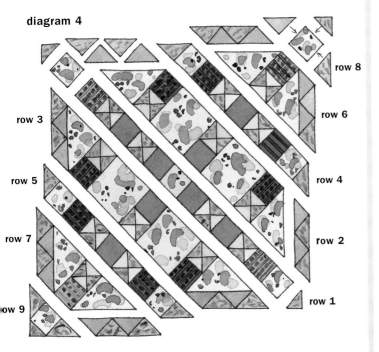

6 Rows 2 and 3 on either side of centre row are, in effect, double width rows and mirror images of each other. Stitch the quarter square units to the rust and striped small squares. Press the seams, then add them to the large squares ending each row with the large triangles.

7 Rows 4 and 5 are the identical except for the last triangles which form part of the outer border. Following diagram 4, stitch these triangles at the ends of the rows.

8 Stitch rows 6 and 7 together, ending with the large triangles. These are double width rows and mirror image.

9 Rows 8 and 9 are mirror image and are made by stitching border triangles to the small square and adding the corner square last.

10 Piece the remaining outer border triangles together in units of four, taking care not to stretch the seams which will all be on the bias edges. Press carefully and add these border units to the double width rows.

11 Stitch all the rows together working from the centre out, being very careful to match seams.

12 Finally, add the last two corner triangles to each end of row 1. If these triangles are a little too large, trim them to size using a square ruler.

FINISHING

1 Layer the backing, wadding and pieced top and baste ready for quilting. Leave an even amount of wadding and backing fabric around the edges as this will be brought over to the front and used as the edging for the quilt.

2 Machine quilt using thread to match the back and the top of the work. Work from the centre outwards and stitch ¼ in/0.75 cm away from outer edges of small non-striped and large squares and large triangles. The small, striped squares have been left unquilted. Leave the inner border triangles unquilted and outline quilt the short edges of the outer border triangles.

3 Trim away the excess wadding to the same size as the quilt top. Trim the backing leaving ¾ in/2 cm showing.

4 Fold the backing to the front of the quilt, placing raw edge of backing to raw edge of quilt top. Fold over again to form an edging approximately ¼ in/0.75 cm wide, covering raw edges, tack and stitch in place.

Red Sky at Night

Red sky at night, shepherd's delight, red sky in the morning, shepherd's warning: a traditional country saying which forecasts fine or wet weather for the approaching day. This quilt is made from red and blue equilateral triangles and would look very striking when hung on a wall. Sometimes working with these triangles may seem rather daunting but instructions are given for a quick cutting technique and some tips are given for matching the points when seaming the triangles together, which should help.

MATERIALS

All fabrics used in the quilt top are 60 in/150 cm wide, 100% cotton

Red stripe: 28 in/70 cm
Blue stripe: 28 in/70 cm
Surprise fabrics: two 6 x 6 in/15 x 15 cm squares of blue and of red striped fabric different from the two above (optional)
Backing and binding: plain red, 40 x 41 in/ 100 x 102 cm for backing and 24 x 24 in/60 x 60 cm for binding
Tracing paper: one A4 sheet
Wadding: lightweight, 40 x 41 in/100 x 102 cm
Coton à broder: red

Quilt size: 36½ x 37½ in/94 x 96 cm

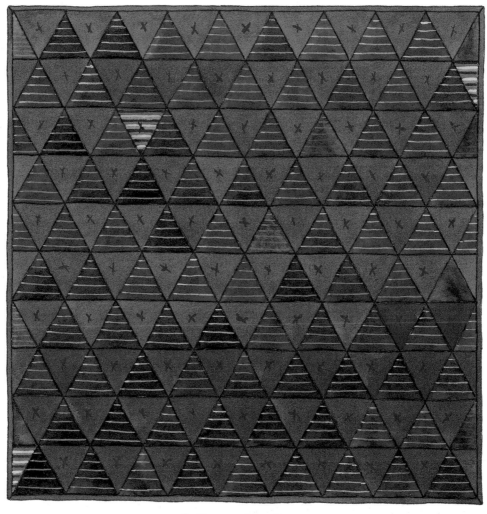

Quilt assembly diagram

CUTTING AND STITCHING

1 Red and blue stripes, place the two fabrics, right sides together and cut nine strips 4½ x 60 in/ 11.5 x 152 cm through both thicknesses.

2 Keeping the fabrics in pairs, right sides together, stitch each pair of strips along both long edges, taking the usual ¼ in/0.75 cm seam allowance.

3 Using the 60 degree angle on your ruler cut 79 pairs of equilateral triangles (diagram 1).

diagram 1

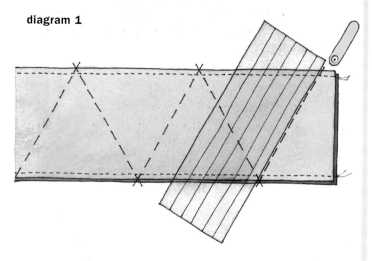

4 These units will be stitched across the points but can easily be pulled apart. Press all the seams open but it is important that you don't cut away the excess fabric. These overhanging points can be used to help you match the seams when putting the units together (diagram 2).

diagram 2

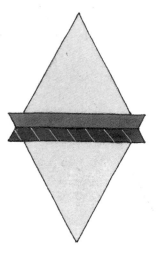

5 From red and blue striped fabric, cut one more set of strips 4½ x 60 in/11.5 x 152 cm, this time leaving the long edges unstitched. Keeping the two strips together, cut nine more pairs of triangles as before. These will be used for the top and bottom rows of the quilt.

Optional: If all the triangles are made from just two fabrics then the design will be very predictable. If you wish to add a little more interest to the quilt, then you could exchange some of the triangles for some "surprise" triangles cut from 6 x 6 in/15 x 15 cm pieces of different stripes. With right sides together stitch two of the different striped red and blue fabrics together, along one edge only. Use one of your existing, cut triangles as a template and cut. Press the seam open.

6 Stitch pairs together to form diagonal rows, taking care to match the triangle points (diagram 3).

diagram 3

7 Add the single triangles, red to the top and blue to the bottom of rows where required (diagram 4). Press the seams open.

diagram 4

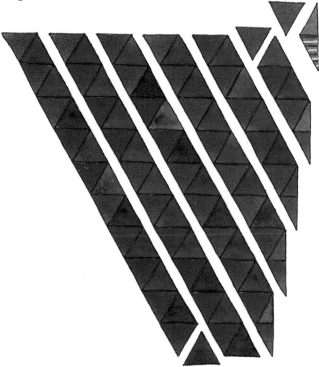

8 To make the half triangles for the side edges, cut a 5 x 9 in/13 x 25 cm strip in both red and blue, layer and stitch along both long sides as before.

9 Trace the template given for half triangles below and using this placed beneath the ruler, cut five facing one direction (diagram 5) and five in the opposite direction.

diagram 5

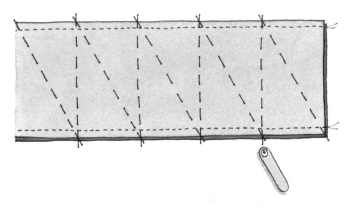

10 Press the seams open and stitch these units to the ends of the rows at the sides as required, referring back to diagram 4.

11 When all diagonal rows have been completed, stitch them together as follows. To match the points, begin by pinning either side of the seams and stitch over the join for approximately 1 in/2.5 cm only. Check that all points meet, if any of them are not exact it will only be necessary to unpick 1 in/2.5 cm of stitching. Now stitch the whole length of the row from beginning to end. Press all the seams open.

FINISHING

1 Layer the backing, wadding and quilt top and baste ready for tying. Mark a spot in the centre of each red triangle and using red coton à broder, make ties in the centre of each.

2 Make the double bias binding 2 in/5 cm wide from the 24 in/60 cm square of plain red, using the continuous strip method. Use to bind the edges with a double fold binding, mitred at the corners.

Templates

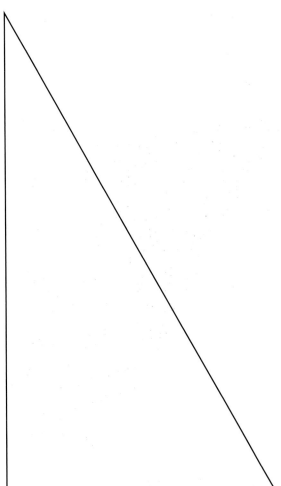

imperial

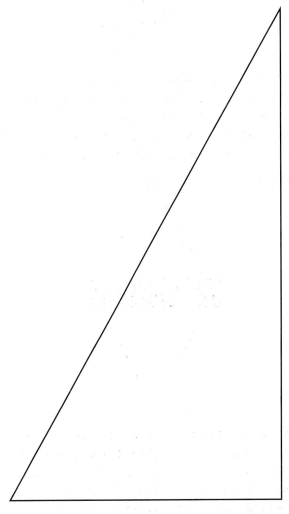

Metric

FLANNEL AND FLASH

Jenni Dobson

Have you, like me, enjoyed the soft, cosy touch of a quilt made with brushed cottons and flannels? Or perhaps your eye has been lured by the gleam of 1930s satin whole-cloth quilts in exhibitions? Wouldn't it be great to have both these attractions in the same quilt? With the quilts in this chapter you can!

The surface texture of quilts is part of their appeal to me. It can come from the quilting or many kinds of embellishment but of course the fabric is the first point at which you can experiment with the surface. Exactly how much variety you can achieve is partly down to what you can find, so widen your search for fabrics to include dress and furnishing fabric departments as well as your regular quilting shops. I hope you will derive as much pleasure from the process of working with such sensual fabrics as I did – and the finished quilts all possess surfaces to delight the eyes and the fingers!

Bright Red Hopes

A new take on the classic red and white combination, this quilt makes a stunning throw for a contemporary style of sofa!

When planning this first design in the collection, I thought initially of country girls who probably wore a lot of red flannel. As the twentieth century progressed and the idea of wearing white for weddings became more usual, for many women this would be their only chance to wear something like white satin. So here in the quilt, white satin flashes against red cotton flannel. Their contrast is bridged by the softer gleam of a striped silk but you could choose a second flannel fabric if you preferred the softer surface. I chose a traditional American block which I had initially identified only by a reference number but when I looked up the name, I discovered it is called "Bright Hopes". How auspicious for a project whose colour scheme was inspired by marriage.

MATERIALS
All fabrics used in the quilt top are 45 in/115 cm wide
Seam allowances are ¼ in/0.75 cm

White satin: 1⅓ yards/1.25 metres
Red flannel/brushed cotton: 1 yard/1 metre
Red striped silk: 1 yard/1 metre
Wadding: lightweight, 52 x 52 in/132 x 132 cm
Backing: 52 x 52 in/132 x 132 cm
Invisible monofilament thread for quilting

Quilt size: 48 x 48 in/120 x 120 cm
Finished block size: 8 in/20 cm square

Note:
Many satins or taffetas today are synthetic, made of acetate or polyester rather than silk. This affects the temperature for pressing. Before they actually stick to the iron, some polyester satins can shrink slightly under a little too much heat. This will cause distortion to your block.

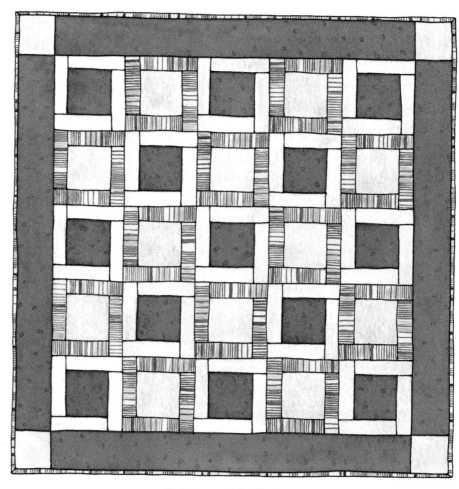

Quilt assembly diagram

ALTERNATIVE COLOURWAYS

The first example (top left) shows the red printed flannel and white satin in the first Bright Hopes quilt accented with black silk for a bold, striking look. The next variation (top right) also starts with a soft print fabric in the centre square but silks pick up its three main colours. Using the yellow twice as often as the other colours keeps the scheme bright. In the third version (bottom left) each of the varied soft plaids from the "Spring Sunshine" quilt is framed with related silk or satin to make a rainbow of squares. Rainbow colours are so popular that I don't apologize for offering another (bottom right): this variation is clean, cool and charming.

CUTTING

● **White satin**, cut 12 squares each 5½ x 5½ in/
13.5 x 13.5 cm;
cut 52 strips each 7 x 2 in/17.5 x 5.5 cm;
cut 4 corner squares for the border each 4½ x
4½ in/11.5 x 11.5 cm.
● **Red flannel**, cut 4 border strips each 40½ x
4½ in/103 x 11.5 cm;
cut 13 squares each 5½ x 5½ in/13.5 x 13.5 cm.
● **Red striped silk**, cut 48 strips each 7 x 2 in/
17.5 x 5.5 cm. I cut mine so the stripes ran across the
strips. Make sure to cut yours to make most effective
use of the fabric you have;
cut the binding from the remaining silk later.

STITCHING

Making a Bright Hopes test block
1 With a red flannel square right side up, place a white
satin strip right side down over the righthand edge and
with the top edges level. The strip will extend beyond the
lower edge of the red square. Stitch the seam about
halfway down the side of the square (diagram 1). Press
the top part of the seam only, away from the centre.

2 Rotate the block so that what was the top edge is
now the righthand side. Place a second white satin strip
over this edge, with the top edges level. This time the
strip fits the edge. Stitch the complete seam (diagram
2). Press the seam away from the centre.

diagram 1   **diagram 2**

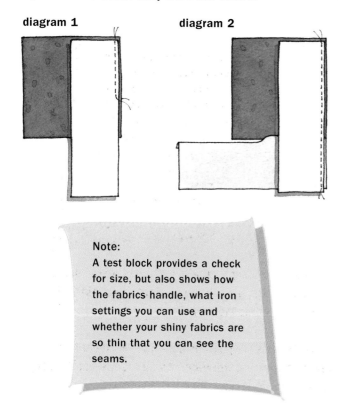

Note:
A test block provides a check
for size, but also shows how
the fabrics handle, what iron
settings you can use and
whether your shiny fabrics are
so thin that you can see the
seams.

3 Rotate again to bring what was the top to the righthand
side and repeat step 2 to add a third strip (diagram 3).
Press away from the centre.

4 Rotate the block once more and add a fourth strip in
the same manner, lifting the tail of strip 1 out of the way
to do so (diagram 4).

diagram 3   **diagram 4**

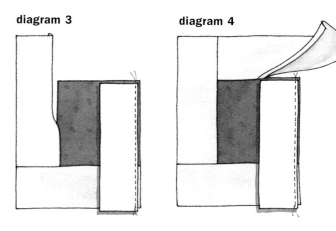

5 Now return to the first seam. Make sure the edges are
matching, then finish stitching the seam over the fourth
strip to the edge of the block (diagram 5). Press carefully.
The block should measure 8½ in/21.5 cm square.

diagram 5

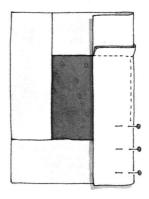

6 In the same way, make a test block with a white satin
centre square and four striped silk framing strips. As
my fabric had an irregular stripe pattern, I decided to
have all four strips on a block with the same pattern.

7 After making both test blocks, make a total of thirteen
with red flannel centres and twelve with white satin
centres. Chain piecing will speed up the block-making. To
do this, stitch the first strip to each centre in the set,
then press them all before adding the second strip, and
so forth. However, working my striped blocks in pairs was
almost as quick, if you prefer this approach. Check the
sizes of your blocks before proceeding to ensure they will
fit together. Over-sized blocks may be trimmed slightly.

ASSEMBLING THE QUILT TOP

1 Following the quilt assembly diagram on page 44, lay out the blocks in a grid of five rows of five blocks, beginning with a red flannel centre square block.

2 Beginning on the first row, pick up the first two blocks and stitch them together, then stitch blocks three and four together. Next join these two pairs and add block five to the end. Press the seams towards the blocks framed in the red striped silk.

3 Assemble rows two to five in the same way, always pressing seams behind the red striped silk. (This means that seams will interlock when the rows are joined.)

4 Place rows one and two, right sides together. Match the block seams together first and pin, then pin in between before stitching. Repeat to join rows three and four. Next join these pairs of rows and finally add row five. I pressed these long horizontal seams open.

ADDING THE BORDERS

1 Measure the pieced top across the middle in both directions to determine the exact length of border required. Mark the vertical length on two of the red flannel borders. Divide both the border and the quilt edges into half then quarters, marking with pins, then with rights sides together, position the borders on the vertical sides of the centre, matching the pins. Pin in between, easing the edges together if needed (diagram 6).

diagram 6

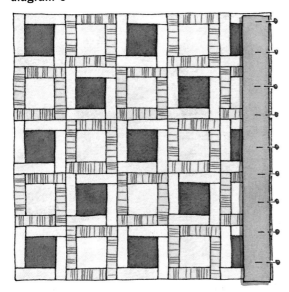

2 Stitch the vertical side borders in place. Press seams towards the border. Trim away the excess border fabric.

3 Stitch one white satin square to one end of the remaining two border strips. Measure the determined horizontal length of red border, then position and stitch on the second white satin square at the other end. Press and check for fit at top and lower edges of the quilt centre. If necessary remove and reposition the second corner square before trimming the excess border fabric.

4 Divide the borders and quilt edges into half and quarters, then position together and stitch as before. Press the seams towards the borders.

FINISHING

1 Spread the backing right side down on a flat surface, then smooth the wadding and the quilt top, right side up on top. Fasten together with safety pins or baste in a grid. Using invisible monofilament thread, machine quilt in lines following the block outlines. Complete with quilting "in-the-ditch" where the border is attached continuing across where the corner patches fit. Check the quilt is straight at the sides and true at the corners, trimming if necessary.

2 Insert a line of permanent tacking within the seam allowance all round the edge of the quilt.

3 From the leftover red striped silk, cut enough binding strips, 2⅜ in/6 cm wide, to fit the perimeter of the quilt, plus 8 - 10 in/20 - 25 cm.

> **Note:**
> In order to use the stripe at right angles to the edge, I had to cut shorter lengths from my remaining fabric than if I had used the stripes along the binding. This caused more joins but I felt that was acceptable for the appearance. I made straight joins (rather than the usual diagonal ones) to preserve the pattern and pressed the seams open.

4 Press the binding in half lengthwise, wrong sides together. Use to bind the edges with a double-fold binding, mitred at the corners.

5 If wished, hand quilt hearts in the block centres, drawing the shape freehand. Add a label and a hanging sleeve if appropriate.

Corn Crib

The warm yellows, creams and gold that inspired the name of this quilt are enhanced by the cool brilliance of turquoise. Together they make a cover suitable for either a boy or a girl. I called it Corn Crib because, besides a "crib" being a safe place for a baby to sleep, a "corn crib" was an American name for a place to store corn.

The challenge of finding a good mix of soft and shiny fabrics for this project was met with quite a few pieces from my years of sewing for my family. The best effect comes from always pairing a shiny-looking fabric with a soft one, regardless of what the actual fibre might be. Sometimes, both fabrics are silk, say, with one of them dull and speckled like calico and the other a glossy stripe. The contrast of surface catching the light is more important than which fibres you have used together. This effect is also increased by using quite a lofty 2 oz wadding inside the quilt.

MATERIALS

All fabrics used in the quilt top are 45 in/115 cm wide
Seam allowances are ¼ in/0.75 cm

Assorted scraps for patchwork: minimum 5 x 3½ in/ 13 x 9 cm (enough for two rectangles in a single four-patch block); maximum 30 x 3½ in/78 x 9 cm (enough for six matching four-patch blocks). See cutting instructions on page 50 for details. You need two contrasting fabrics for each set of blocks: I used variations of cream for the contrast fabrics.
Cream novelty weave: 20 in/50 cm for border
Cotton flannel: 9 in/20 cm for binding
Wadding: 2 oz, 38 x 46 in/95 x 115 cm
Backing: 38 x 46 in/95 x 115 cm
Invisible monofilament thread for quilting

Quilt size: 36 x 44 in/90 x 110 cm

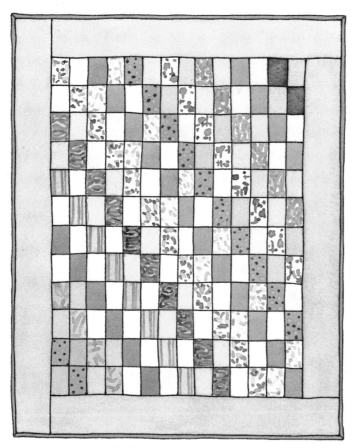

Quilt assembly diagram

Note:
When fabrics are too thin or very slippery or fray easily, you can iron the lightest weight iron-on interfacing to the reverse side. This adds stability and opacity without spoiling their appearance or making them difficult to sew.

CUTTING

Note:
To cut satin or silk successfully with a rotary cutter always fit a new blade!

● **Assorted scraps,** the four-patch blocks are made in sets of identical blocks: two different sets of six identical blocks, two sets of five the same, etc. down to two separate and different single blocks in opposite corners. Before cutting, plan which pairs of fabrics you will use for which sets, according to how much you have of each fabric. I began by cutting strips for the 6-block sets as they needed most fabric:

for the 6-block sets, cut one strip 30 x 3½ in/78 x 9 cm of each of two contrasting fabrics
for the 5-block sets, cut strips 25 x 3½ in/65 x 9 cm;
for the 4-block sets, cut strips 20 x 3½ in/52 x 9 cm;
for the 3-block sets, cut strips 15 x 3½ in/39 x 9 cm;
for the 2-block sets, cut strips 10 x 3½ in/26 x 9 cm;
for the single blocks, cut strips 5 x 3½ in/13 x 9 cm.

● **Border fabric,** cut four border strips each 37 x 4½ in/ 103 x 11.5 cm.

Note:
The border on the quilt shown was cut differently because I was working with a leftover piece. You do not need to copy my arrangement though it shows that variations are always possible if the fabric dictates.

● **Binding,** cut four strips 1⅛ in/3 cm wide across the width of the fabric for the binding.

STITCHING
Making a rectangular four-patch block

Note:
Please make a test block with spare fabric before you start on those for your quilt.

1 To make a test block, cut two contrasting strips, each 5 x 3½ in/13 x 9 cm. With right sides facing, stitch them together down the longer side (diagram 1). Press the seam towards the darker fabric.

2 Cut across the pieced strips to make two 2½ in/6.5 cm wide slices. Turn one around to make the alternating characteristic four-patch pattern and join (diagram 2). This block should measure 4½ x 6½ in/11.5 x 16.5 cm. If not, check your seam allowance. However, as long as all your blocks are consistent, they will fit together. Once satisfied with the test, proceed to make sets of blocks.

diagram 1

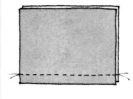

diagram 2

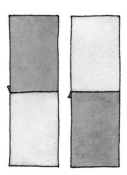

3 To make sets of blocks, you will be stitching longer strips together and cross-cutting them into more slices, e.g. four slices for two blocks; six slices for three blocks, etc. The slices are always 2½ in/6.5 cm wide.

ASSEMBLING THE QUILT TOP

1 The quilt uses a grid of six rows of seven blocks, with the different permutations moving diagonally across on successive rows. Follow the quilt assembly diagram on page 48 to lay out the blocks.

2 Be sure to keep the sequence correct when stitching the rows of blocks together. Beginning on the first row, pick up the first two blocks and stitch them together. Then stitch blocks three and four together, then five and six. Next join the first two pairs and then add block seven to the third pair. Join these units together and press. Press the seams open.

3 Assemble rows two to six in the same way, always pressing as you go.

4 Now join rows one and two, matching the block seams together first and pressing after stitching. Repeat to join the remaining rows into pairs. Next join these pairs of rows to complete the top and give a final press.

ADDING THE BORDERS

1 Measure the pieced top across the middle in both directions to determine the exact length of border required. Mark the vertical length on two of the borders. Divide both the border and the quilt edges into half then quarters, marking with pins, then with right sides together, position the borders on the vertical sides of the centre, matching the pins. Pin in between, easing the edges together if needed (diagram 3). (Often the edge of the top can seem a little longer than the centre measurement. Easing the border on in this way reduces the chances of your quilt finishing with a wavy edge!)

diagram 3

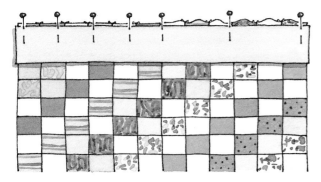

2 Stitch the vertical side borders in place. Press the seams towards the borders. Check they fit properly, then trim away the excess border fabric.

3 Add the top and bottom borders in the same way.

FINISHING

1 Spread the backing right side down on a flat surface, then smooth the wadding and the quilt top, right side up on top. Fasten together with safety pins or baste in a grid. Using invisible monofilament thread, machine quilt diagonally through the blocks. I also quilted round where the borders are attached. Check the quilt is straight at the sides and true at the corners, trimming if necessary.

2 Insert permanent tacking within the seam allowance around the edge of the quilt.

3 Join the binding strips and use to bind the edges with a single-fold binding, mitred at the corners.

4 Add a label and a hanging sleeve if appropriate.

Hearth and Home

The design of this cot quilt owes much to the country tradition of frame quilts. Here there is a quilted centre square surrounded by two frames. The inner frame uses another country method – the "hit 'n miss" approach to strip piecing – combined with log cabin blocks in the corners. The simpler outer frame echoes the inner with log cabin blocks in the corners connecting plain cut rectangles of border fabric.

A floral printed Viyella in pink determined the colour scheme for the whole quilt, with the varied pinks, blue-violet and greys being picked out from the scrap collection. Choosing a main border fabric first with this purpose in mind makes good sense but you need not use every colour in the print elsewhere in the quilt. Nor need you be restricted to only those colours. Something which bridges the existing colours or contrasts with them may work well. I also enjoyed finding a mixture of textures for the scrap collection in this project.

MATERIALS

All fabrics used in the quilt top are 45 in/115 cm wide
Seam allowances are ¼ in/0.75 cm

Pink striped or checked silk: 20 in/50 cm
Pink silk: 19 x 19 in/48.5 x 48.5 cm square
Pink printed Viyella or cotton flannel: 27 in/70 cm
Assorted scraps of silk, cotton flannels: a total of 1 yard/1 metre
Backing: 55 in/140 cm
Wadding: lightweight, 45 x 45 in/115 x 115 cm

Quilt size: 42½ x 42½ in/108 x 108 cm

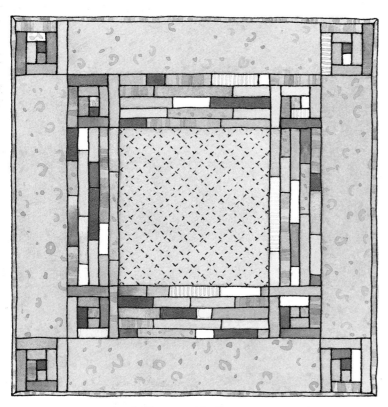

Quilt assembly diagram

Note:
Always use a new blade for rotary cutting delicate fabrics like satin and silk and always put a new needle in your machine to avoid snagging. Also clean the bobbin case more often when sewing flannels.

CUTTING

● **Pink print**, cut 4 strips for borders each 31 x 6½ in/ 79 x 17 cm;

from leftovers, cut a few strips 1¾ in/4.75 cm wide to include in the strip patchwork.

● **Assorted scraps**, cut 2 sets of 4 centres each 1¾ in/4.75 cm square for the log cabin blocks. I chose different fabrics for the centres for the inner border from those for the outer border;

cut strips 1¾ in/4.75 cm wide and of varied length for the log cabin blocks and "hit 'n miss" borders.

● **Pink striped silk**, cut 4 strips 2⅜ in/6 cm wide across the full width of the fabric, plus an extra half strip for binding;

from the remainder, cut a few strips 1¾ in/4.75 cm wide and varied length for the strip patchwork.

● **Backing**, cut a square as wide as the width of the fabric. This will be approximately 45 in/115 cm; the remainder can be used to make a hanging sleeve.

PREPARATION FOR QUILT-AS-YOU-GO

1 You need to position the centre of the quilt correctly over the backing and wadding in order to be sure you can piece the whole top without 'running out' of backing. For this reason take the time to prepare the layers carefully. Fold a diagonal in both directions on the backing fabric. Press lightly so you can see the fold without stretching it. These mark the centre.

2 Place the wadding on a flat surface and centre the backing over it, right side up, so you can see the folds. Now using coloured thread, tack the two layers together along the diagonals. I found it easier to work four lines from the centre outwards towards each corner, then tack the layers together thoroughly using a paler thread. When you turn the layer over with wadding side upper-most, you should be able to see clearly the diagonal coloured tacking that marks the centre.

STITCHING

1 Begin by marking a diagonal 2 in/5 cm quilting grid on the right side of the pink silk square for the centre.

2 Centre this silk, right side up, over the marked middle of the wadding and backing. Pin and tack.

diagram 1

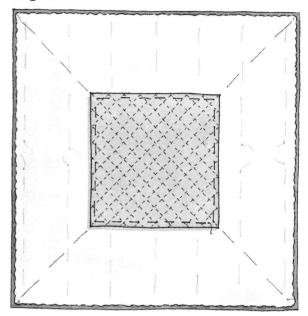

3 Machine quilt through all layers. Start with the two main diagonals, then work outwards from them, one line each side in each direction until the quilting is complete (diagram 1). Set aside until needed.

4 Next work eight log cabin blocks using the scrap strips. To make one block: following the numbering in diagram 2, place a strip 1, right sides together, to one side of the centre square and stitch (diagram 3). Press and trim.

diagram 2

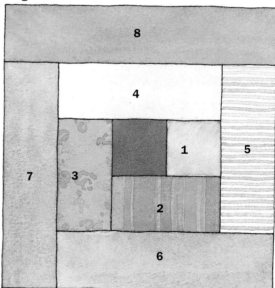

diagram 3

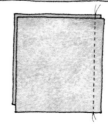

5 In the same way stitch strip 2 across the end of strip 1 and the centre square, then press (diagram 4). Proceed working your way round two full circuits of the centre. You may like to work the blocks in pairs. It does not matter for this country style of quilt if the strips look a little uneven. In fact with varied fabric types this is quite likely to happen and adds to the character.

diagram 4

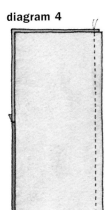

6 Now work four inner "hit 'n miss" borders using strips left from the Log Cabin blocks. Assemble pieces of varied length into strips about 26 in/66 cm long. Join five strips of this length to make one border (diagram 5).

diagram 5

7 Place one "hit 'n miss" border right sides together along one side of the quilted centre, aligning raw edges. The border should be a bit longer than required. Pin, then stitch into place (diagram 6).

diagram 6

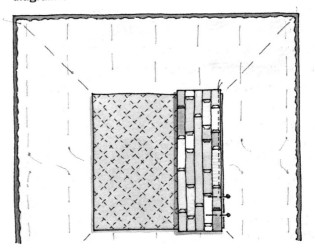

8 Flip the border right side up into position over the wadding and press the seam lightly. Using scissors, trim the ends level with the centre and pin or tack the long edge to the quilt layers. Repeat to add a second border to the opposite side of the centre square.

9 Stitch one Log Cabin block to one end of both remaining "hit 'n miss" borders and press. Now test the borders against the remaining sides of the centre to establish the correct position for the remaining Log Cabin blocks. Stitch them in position, press and check the fit before trimming the excess border length.

10 Stitch these units to the opposite sides of the centre square in the same way as before, this time matching the block joins with the seams for the first borders. Pin or tack the long edges to the quilt layers.

11 In the same way, add two outer borders of pink print, then make two border-plus-blocks units for the remaining sides and attach. Pin the edges ready for binding.

FINISHING

1 Check that the corners of the quilt are square and true, then insert permanent tacking within the seam allowance around the edge of the quilt. Trim the excess wadding and backing level with the pieced top.

2 Following step 3 of "Finishing" for "Bright Red Hopes" on page 47, bind the edges with a double-fold binding, mitred at the corners.

3 Add a label and hanging sleeve if you wish.

Bright Hopes Fulfilled

Having seen the "Bright Hopes" block worked in the strong contrast of red and white, I thought it would be interesting to see how it looked using low contrast. The subtle palette of assorted white, cream and stone allows the eye to concentrate on and enjoy the differences of surface. This fabric collection, again with some dressmaking leftovers, includes damask, raw silk, shantung, silk noil, Viyella, moiré, a watered silk furnishing fabric with a woven figure and silk with a pre-stitched grid as used for wedding gowns. To ensure adequate variety, try to collect between 12 and 16 different fabrics. Here each block features five different fabrics, one for each of the pieces. I chose to bind the edge with a raw silk version of the same shade of silk as used for the setting to keep the texture subtle. The quilt-as-you-stitch construction using vertical columns of blocks will still make assembling and finishing this little quilt or wallhanging speedy.

MATERIALS

As you are working with a wide variety of fabrics, note that their widths may vary. For the patchwork, 7 in/18 cm of any fabric should be adequate
Seam allowances are ¼ in/0.75 cm

Assorted scraps: in white, cream, stone; minimum size scrap 7 in/18 cm square or equivalent, in total equivalent to about 1⅓ yards/1.2 metres
Off-white silk: 20 in/50 cm for settings
Off-white raw silk: 10 in/25 cm for binding
Wadding: low loft or needle-punched, 40 x 36 in/ 100 x 90 cm
Backing: 40 x 36 in/100 x 90 cm
Thread for sewing and quilting

Quilt size: 36 x 28 in/90 x 70 cm

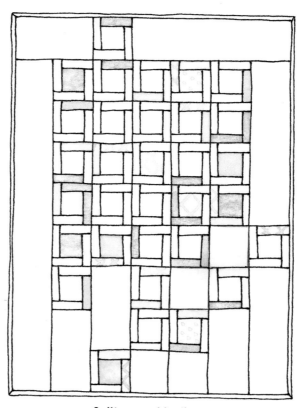

Quilt assembly diagram

CUTTING

● **Assorted scraps,**

to ensure variety for the blocks, cut 2 squares each 3 x 3 in/7.5 x 7.5 cm and 2 sets of 4 strips 1¼ x 3¾ in/3.5 x 9.5 cm from each fabric, then check how many units you have and if necessary cut a few more squares and sets to make enough for 32 blocks.

● **Off-white silk,** cut setting strips as follows:

1 strip 32½ x 4½ in/81.5 x 11.5 cm;

2 strips 16½ x 4½ in/41.5 x 11.5 cm;

1 strip 12½ x 4½ in/ 31.5 x 11.5 cm;

4 strips 8½ x 4½/21.5 x 11.5 cm;

cut 4 squares each 4½ x 4½ in/11.5 x 11.5 cm.

● **Raw silk,** for the binding cut enough strips 1½ in/4 cm wide for the perimeter of the quilt, plus 8-10 in/20-25 cm.

STITCHING

Making a Bright Hopes block

> Note:
> Please make a test block before you start on those for your quilt.

1 Follow the instructions for making the test block on page 46 of "Bright Red Hopes" quilt but use the smaller patches required for this project. You will find that the first partly-stitched seam will be very short and it is possible that as you add the strips around the centre square, the first strip will be pressed awkwardly. Therefore, before returning to complete stitching the first seam, press the block again with the strip correctly placed. This makes it easier to stitch neatly and makes wobbles or puckers less likely.

2 After making a test block, proceed to make a total of 32 blocks. Mix up the strips to ensure that you don't stitch strips onto a centre of the same fabric.

3 Check the sizes of your blocks before proceeding to ensure they will fit together. Over-sized blocks may be trimmed slightly.

ASSEMBLING THE QUILT

1 The quilt-as-you-stitch assembly uses a grid of seven vertical columns of blocks, setting strips and squares, with a horizontal row across the top. The blocks are arranged with single ones in the outer settings, so that an effect of a frame is achieved. Follow the quilt assembly diagram on page 56 or experiment with the arrangement of your blocks until you are happy. Remember that you can turn each block four different ways so plenty of permutations are available!

2 Join each vertical column of blocks and settings into a strip, being sure to keep the sequence correct and press the seams. Join the settings and block for the top horizontal row, then press.

3 Press the backing fabric and spread, right side down, on a flat surface with the wadding on top. Tack these layers together, marking the centre vertically and horizontally as you go (diagram 1).

diagram 1

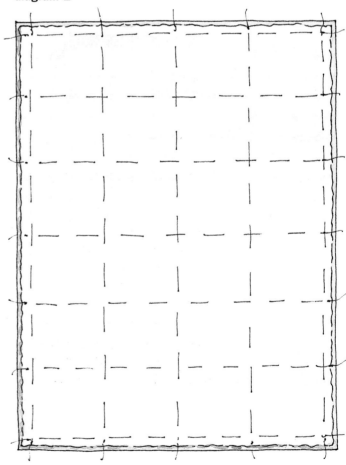

4 Place the middle column of blocks in the centre of the wadding, right side up, keeping the top block far enough down from the top edge of the backing layers to allow for the top row to be added last. Check that it is straight and parallel to the sides of the backing before you pin or tack in place along both edges (diagram 2).

diagram 2

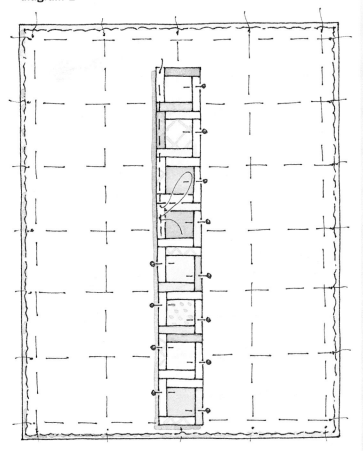

5 Place the column of blocks which will appear on the righthand side of the middle column, right side down, all edges level with the first column and pin down the right-hand side. Stitch through all layers, thus quilting at the same time. Flip right side up into place and press lightly. Avoid compressing the wadding with too much heat.

6 Pin the free edge ready for positioning the next strip, right side down over it and attaching in the same way. Repeat the process to add three columns to each side of the centre strip.

7 Pin or tack down the long edges of the outer side strips, then place the top row, right side down over the top end of the columns and stitch (diagram 3). Flip right side up and press before tacking the outer edge. Check that the corners of the quilt are true and the sides straight, then trim away excess backing and wadding. Remove the tacking from the back.

diagram 3

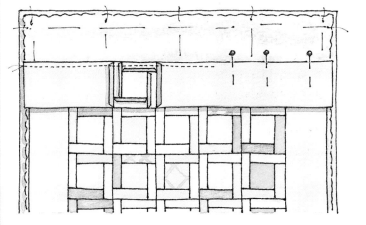

FINISHING

1 If using raw silk to bind as I did, using double binding will make the task easier. The folded edge will stitch in place to finish without fraying. Join the strips and press the seams open. Press the binding in half lengthwise, wrong sides together. Use to bind the edges with a double-fold binding, mitred at the corners.

2 Add a label and a hanging sleeve if appropriate.

Spring Sunshine

Collections of flannel fabrics are often rather muted in colour, well suited to making cuddly, warm winter projects. However, I was lucky enough to find these wonderful directional flannels in what I think of as confectionery colours. They are more colourful than pastels but not overpoweringly bright. Besides looking good enough to eat, they also reminded me of spring flowers and so seemed perfect for a quilt to warm up those chilly days of early spring. The light yellow silk accent fabric prompted the quilt title. The flannels aren't suitable for cutting into small pieces, so a design of chunky rectangles arranged in a "Trip Around the World" design is suitably bold and speedy to execute.

MATERIALS

Note that flannel fabrics may be up to 60 in/150 cm wide and if so, you may be able to reduce quantities Seam allowances are ¼ in/0.75 cm

Silk in an accent colour picked out from the flannels: 1 yard/1 metre
Flannel checks or plaids: 20 in/50 cm of each of seven different colourways
Wadding: lightweight, 70 x 49 in/175 x 123 cm
Backing: 70 x 49 in/175 x 123 cm
Invisible monofilament thread for quilting

Quilt size: 66 x 45 in/165 x 113 cm

Quilt assembly diagram

CUTTING

Before cutting, arrange the flannel fabrics in your chosen sequence and number them 1 to 7. The silk fabric will be no. 8. I taped swatches to a numbered card to record my plan.

● **Silk**, working lengthwise, i.e. parallel to the selvage, cut 4 strips, 26 x 3½ in/60 x 7.5 cm; cut 2 strips, 13 x 3½ in/30 x 7.5 cm; cut 5 rectangles, 6½ x 3½ in/15 x 7.5 cm; if using for binding to finish ½ in/1.5 cm wide, cut 6 strips across the width of the fabric, each 2⅝ in/6.75 cm wide. The measurements include a little extra to accommodate the thickness of the wadding in the bound edge.

● **Flannel**, from fabrics 1 and 2, cut 5 strips, 26 x 3½ in/60 x 7.5 cm and 1 strip, 13 x 3½ in/30 x 7.5 cm; from fabric 3, cut 5 strips, 26 x 3½ in/60 x 7.5 cm; from fabrics 4, 5 and 6, cut 4 strips, 26 x 3½ in/60 x 7.5 cm, 1 strip, 13 x 3½ in/30 x 7.5 cm and 2 rectangles, 6½ x 3½ in/15 x 7.5 cm; from fabric 7, cut 4 strips, 26 x 3½ in/60 x 7.5 cm and 2 strips, 13 x 3½ in/30 x 7.5 cm; for an alternative binding, strips can be cut later from the leftovers.

STITCHING

1 The most efficient method to work a top like this is to make sets of strips which are then cross-cut into slices. Each set will make four slices of the design, one for each quarter of the quilt, except for row F which only makes two slices, one for each side of the centre. The separate rectangles which you have cut will fit down the middle of the quilt to complete the centre symmetry of the design.

2 For row A, stitch together along the long edges, in the correct numerical sequence, one 26 in/60 cm strip of fabrics 1 to 7. Press the seams, then cross-cut into four slices, each 6½ in/15 cm wide. Label each slice as "row A" (diagram 1).

> **Note:**
> Sets for B to E will cross-cut into four slices except for a short set B (fabrics 7 and 8) which will cut into two slices.

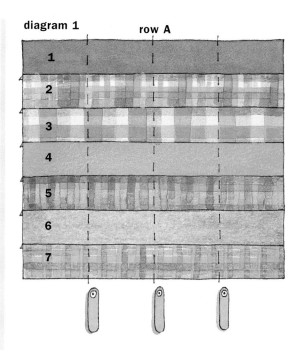

diagram 1   row A

3 Being careful to keep the sequence correct through all subsequent sets, make and label sets in the same manner, as follows:
row B, one long strip of fabrics 1 to 6, cross-cut into four slices as before and a set of one 13 in/30 cm strip of fabrics 7 and 8, cross-cut into two slices (diagram 2);

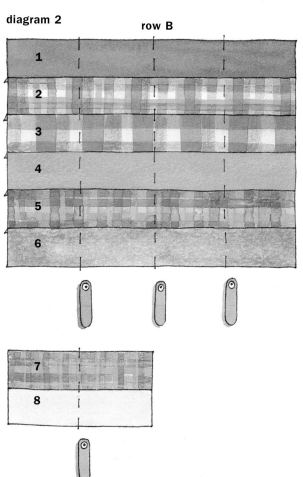

diagram 2   row B

row C, one long strip of fabrics 1 to 5 and a second set using one long strip each of 7 and 8, both cross-cut into four slices as before;

row D, one long strip of fabrics 1 to 4 and a second set using one long strip each of 6 to 8, both cross-cut into four slices as before;

row E, one long strip of fabrics 1 to 3 and a second set using one long strip each of 5 to 8, both cross-cut into four slices as before;

row F, one 13 in/30 cm strip of fabrics 1 and 2 and a second set using one 13 in/30 cm strip of fabrics 4 to 8, both cross-cut into two slices as before (diagram 3).

diagram 3   **row F**

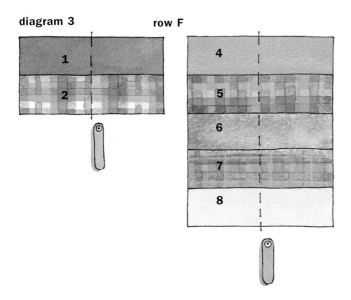

diagram 4

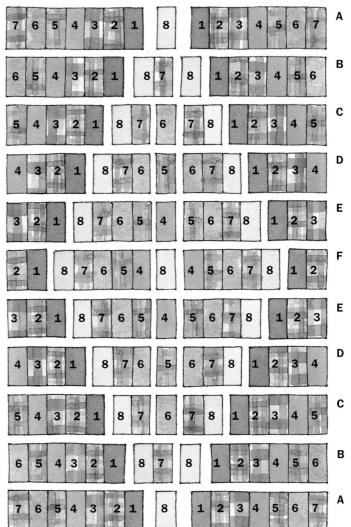

4 Following the layout in diagram 4, arrange the sets in their correct positions. Complete the rows with the individual rectangles, putting the fifth silk rectangle (fabric 8) in the centre.

ASSEMBLING THE QUILT TOP
1 Being careful to keep the design sequence correct, stitch together the pieces in each row across the quilt in turn and press.

2 Next join the rows together. To make this task more manageable, I joined two pairs of rows together at the top and bottom of the quilt and made a unit of three rows in the middle. I chose to press the horizontal seams open. Assemble the three parts to complete the top.

FINISHING
1 Spread the backing right side down on a flat surface, then smooth the wadding and the quilt top, right side up on top. Fasten together with safety pins or baste in a grid. Using invisible monofilament thread, machine quilt the horizontal seams.

2 Check the quilt is straight at the sides and true at the corners. I think a larger quilt suits a wider binding. If you wish to finish with a wider binding as I did, you need to leave an appropriate extra amount of wadding and backing beyond the edge of the top when trimming. For my ½ in/1.5 cm binding, I left an extra ¼ in/0.75 cm beyond the seam allowance on the patches.

3 Insert a line of permanent tacking within the seam allowance all round the edge of the quilt top.

4 If using double binding as I did, join the binding strips with diagonal seams to make a continuous length to fit all round the quilt and use to bind the edges with a double-fold binding, mitred at the corners.

5 Add a label and a hanging sleeve if appropriate.

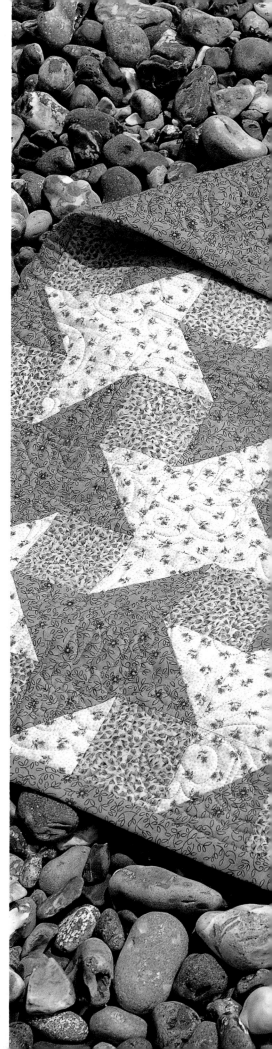

COUNTRY THRIFT

Katharine Guerrier

Recycling scraps of fabric into quilts and home dyeing to create your own unique fabrics have always been a part of many quiltmakers' philosophy. The development of modern tools and techniques means that the conservation of both time and energy can now be added to these traditional ways of extending your resources. Rotary cutting and quick piecing have made it possible to speed up the processes of quiltmaking and opened up exciting new design possibilities. In this collection of quilts I have tried to combine traditional patterns with the freer methods of cutting and piecing, embracing both the old and the new in the hope that you will be inspired to experiment and create your own decorative textiles. Several of the quilts here have also been quilted on a longarm quilting machine, a process for which you don't need to make a quilt "sandwich" (see page 69).

Interlocking Stars

A variation on a classic traditional block, "Friendship Star", made in three harmonizing floral pastels makes a pretty cot quilt for a new baby. The design is completed on a longarm quilting machine.

MATERIALS

All fabrics used in the quilt top are 45 in/115 cm wide, 100% cotton

Floral prints in the following quantities and colours:
White floral print: ¾ yard/75 cm
Blue floral print: 2½ yards/2.25 metres, including backing and binding
Green floral print: ½ yard/50 cm
Wadding: 2 oz or low loft, 36 x 42 in/91 x 106 cm
Machine quilting thread in pale blue

Quilt size: 34 x 40 in/86.5 x 101.5 cm

Quilt assembly diagram

ALTERNATIVE COLOURWAYS

Top left: for the homespun look use a combination of plaids and stripes; top right: three brights used together makes for an attention seeking quilt with a bold combination of colours; bottom left: made in typical Amish plain colours teamed with black, this quilt will make a strong graphic statement; bottom right: red and green Christmas fabrics teamed with a crisp white-on-white print will welcome a Christmas baby .

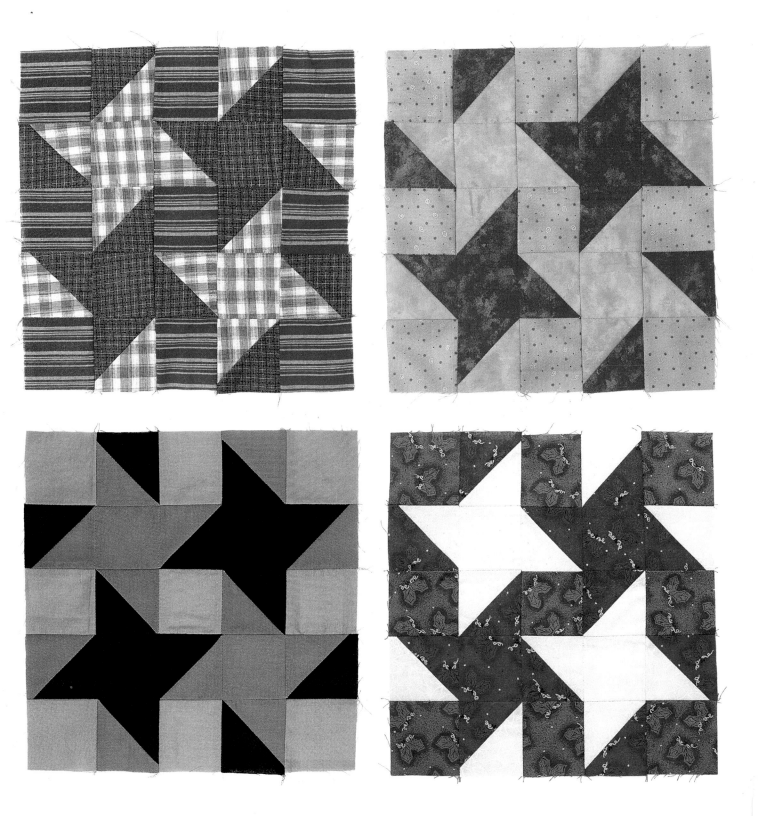

CUTTING

- **White,** cut 36 x 4 in/10 cm squares;
15 x 3½ in/9 cm squares.
- **Blue,** cut 36 x 4 in/10 cm squares;
strips, 4 in/10 cm wide to a total length of 150 in/
381 cm for binding;
1 piece, 36 x 42 in/91 x 106 cm for backing;
15 x 3½ in/9 cm squares.
- **Green,** cut 42 x 3½ in/9 cm squares.

STITCHING

1 Place one white and one blue square right sides
together. Draw one diagonal line from corner to corner
on the wrong side and stitch ¼ in/0.75 cm away on
either side of the line (diagram 1).

diagram 1

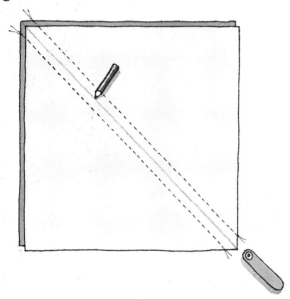

2 Cut apart along the centre line, open out and press.
Repeat with all of the other blue and white 4 in/10cm
squares to make a total of 72 bi-coloured squares.

3 Trim the resulting units to exactly 3½ in/9 cm
squares, making sure that the seam runs from corner
to corner (diagram 2).

diagram 2

4 Working in horizontal rows and following the quilt
assembly diagram on page 66, stitch the plain and
bi-coloured squares together. Then stitch the rows
together, taking care to match seams. Press.

5 Join the 4 in/10 cm binding strips to make one
continuous length.

FINISHING

1 If you plan to do your own quilting, spread the backing right side down on a flat surface, then smooth the
wadding and the quilt top, right side up on top. Fasten
together with safety pins or baste in a grid.

2 Using the "free motion machine quilting" method and
referring to the photograph opposite as a guide for the
design, quilt over the surface of the quilt in pale blue
machine quilting thread.

3 Using the blue binding strip, bind the edges with a
double-fold binding, mitred at the corners.

LONGARM QUILTING MACHINES

The quilt pictured here was quilted by Jenny Spencer of "The Colour Room" using the "Feather Meander" pattern on a longarm quilting machine.

These machines have hundreds of options in the quilting designs available. You can choose edge-to-edge quilting; all-over quilting of one design over the entire quilt, or select a number of patterns to complement each other, e.g. medallions, feathers, cables and cross-hatching, all combined in one quilt. Added to these is the option of quilting to your own freehand style and a choice of decorative threads.

The quilt top, wadding and backing are mounted onto separate rollers which are part of the frame of the machine. This means that the three layers of the quilt need not be tacked together. The quilting is stitched in sections about 24 in/60 cm in width. When the first width is completed the quilt is moved on and the next section is ready to be quilted. The machine is hand operated and takes considerable skill to operate successfully.

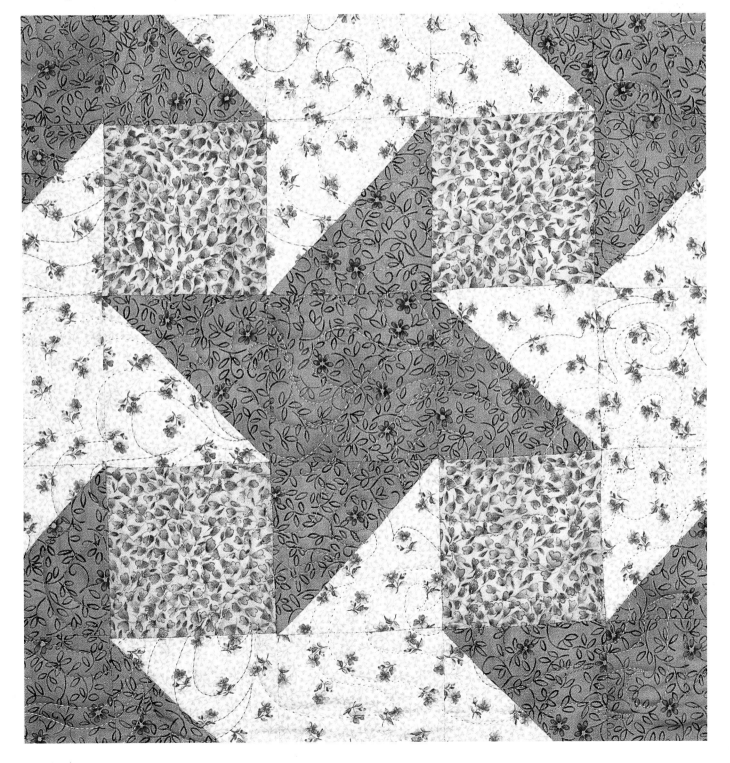

Pioneer Patches

Calico is teamed with plaids and small flower prints giving a nostalgic air to this small lap quilt, reminiscent of earlier times when fabric choices were limited. Using quick piecing techniques, the block centres are constructed in quarter squares of calico and plaids. When the blocks are placed edge to edge, the sawtooth and plain outer strips make a secondary design resembling double sashing. A calico border with bias plaid trim frames the centre panel of the patchwork. Bias plaid in a different colourway is also used for the binding and the design is completed with machine quilting.

MATERIALS

All fabrics used in the quilt top are 45 in/115 cm wide

Calico: 2 yards/2 metres

Cotton plaids: ½ yard/50 cm in total **or** six 9 in/23 cm squares for the blocks plus two fat quarters for border trim and binding

Blue flower print: ¾ yard/75 cm

Backing: cotton, 45 x 54 in/114 x 137 cm

Wadding: 2 oz or low loft, 45 x 54 in/114 x 137 cm

Machine quilting thread in ivory

Quilt size: 41 x 50 in/104 x 127 cm

Quilt assembly diagram

CUTTING

● **Calico, cut the following pieces:**

outer borders: 2 strips, 52 x 4 in/132 x 10.25 cm;
2 strips, 35 x 4in/89 x 10.25 cm;
inner borders: two strips, 44 x 2½ in/112 x 6.25 cm;
2 strips, 35 x 2½ in/89 x 6.25 cm;
6 squares, 7¾ in/19.75 cm;
strips, 2½ in/6.25 cm wide, to a total length of
340 in/864 cm.

● **Plaids,** cut 6 x 7¾ in/19.75 cm squares. Keep the remaining fat quarters for the border trim and binding.

● **Blue flower print,** cut 5 strips across the width of the fabric, 2½ in/6.25 cm wide.

STITCHING

1 Place one plaid square right sides together with one calico square. Press, then mark two diagonal lines across from opposite corners on the wrong side of the calico. Stitch from the centre to the edges, ¼ in/0.75 cm away from the diagonal lines (diagram 1).

diagram 1

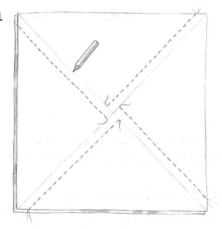

2 Cut across both diagonal lines, open out and press seams towards the plaid fabric. Stitch two of the resulting bi-coloured triangles together to make the block centres (diagram 2). Make 12 altogether.

diagram 2

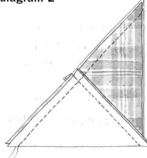

3 Using the random length 2½ in/6.25cm strips of calico, stitch a strip to the top and bottom of each block centre, cutting the lengths to fit as you work (diagram 3). Press.

diagram 3

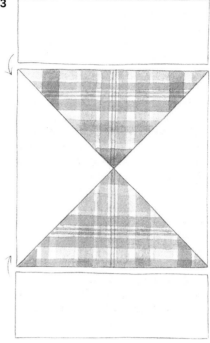

4 Place each of the 2½ in/6.25 cm blue flower print strips right sides together with a calico strip of the same length. Press, then mark out a total of 72 squares, 2½ in/6.25 cm wide along the length. Draw a diagonal line across each square, then stitch ¼ in/0.75 cm away from these diagonal lines on both sides (diagram 4).

diagram 4

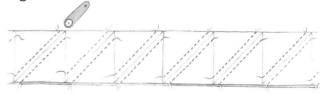

5 Cut the squares apart, then cut along each diagonal line. Open out and press the seams towards the blue print. To make the sawtooth edging, stitch the resulting squares together in strips of six (diagram 5). Make 24 strips altogether.

diagram 5

6 Stitch the sawtooth strips to the remaining two sides of each block, matching seams where necessary, then trim the width of the calico strips level with the outer edge of the sawtooth strips (diagram 6).

diagram 6

7 When all twelve blocks are complete follow the quilt assembly diagram on page 70 and arrange the blocks with the plaid fabrics as desired, then stitch them together. Try to match the sawtooth seams at the points of intersection.

ADDING THE BORDERS

1 For the inner border stitch the 2½ in/6.25 cm strips of calico to the top, bottom and sides, cutting the lengths to fit as you work.

2 To make the plaid trim for the borders, fold the plaid fabric in half diagonally across the bias grain and cut 1 in/2.5 cm wide strips, cutting sufficient length to go around the edges of the calico borders. Join where necessary.

3 Fold the bias strips in half lengthwise, wrong sides together, and tack them to the top, bottom, then each of the sides of the quilt along the edges of the border (diagram 7).

diagram 7

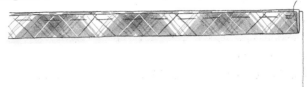

4 For the outer border, stitch the 4 in/10.25 cm wide strips of calico to the top, bottom and sides, aligning raw edges with the raw edges of the bias trim. Stitch with a ¼ in/0.75 cm seam allowance, so that the bias trim is trapped in the seams (diagram 8). Press.

diagram 8

FINISHING

1 Lay out the backing, wadding and pieced top and fasten together with safety pins or baste in a grid.

2 Using the "free motion machine quilting" method and referring to the photograph as a guide for the design, quilt over the surface within the border trim in ivory machine quilting thread. Quilt the borders in straight lines, parallel to the edges. Alternatively, use a longarm quilting machine as for the quilt in the photograph, which was stitched by Jenny Spencer of "The Colour Room" using the "Feather Meander" pattern.

3 Trim the backing and wadding level with the edges of the quilt. From the second fat quarter of plaid fabric cut strips 2½ in/6.25 cm wide and of sufficient length to go all around the outer edges of the quilt. Join the strips where necessary. Fold and press the binding in half lengthwise, wrong sides together and apply as a double-fold binding, mitred at the corners.

Strips and Windmills

This design combines quickly pieced strips of fabric and off-centre pinwheels to give a contemporary assymetrical look for a sofa throw, lap quilt or even pet basket. Bright colours are used in dappled fabrics for both the strips and the windmills. The windmill blocks are teamed with black to accent the bright colours. The top can be pieced in a matter of a few hours and the quilting is done by machine in random zig zags which need no marking.

MATERIALS

All fabrics used in the quilt top are 45 in/115 cm wide, 100% cotton

Mauve, green and yellow: ½ yard/50 cm of each for the strips
Black: ½ yard/50 cm
Medium green: ½ yard/50 cm for the additional pinwheels and binding
Bright red, dark pink, pink, lime green, orange: 6 in/16 cm square of each for the pinwheels;
Wadding: 2 oz or low loft, 48 x 41 in/122 x 104 cm
Backing: cotton, 48 x 41 in/122 x 104 cm
Tracing paper: one A4 sheet
Invisible monofilament quilting thread
Variegated machine embroidery thread

Quilt size: 46 x 39 in/117 x 99 cm

Quilt assembly diagram

CUTTING

- **Yellow**, cut 5 x 3½ in/9 cm strips, across the width of fabric.
- **Mauve and green**, cut 4 x 3½ in/9 cm strips of each, across the width of fabric.
- **Black**, cut 5 x 6 in/16 cm squares and one rectangle, 9 x 6 in/23 x 16 cm.
- **Medium green**, cut 1 rectangle, 9 x 6 in/23 x 16 cm and reserve the remainder for the binding.

STITCHING

1 Place one black square right sides together with one 6 in/16 cm square of each of the bright coloured squares. On the wrong side of the lighter fabrics, mark out four 2¾ in/7 cm squares, then draw a diagonal line across the squares in one direction from corner to corner. Stitch ¼ in/0.75 cm away on either side of this diagonal line (diagram 1).

diagram 1

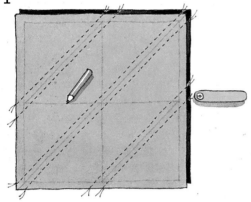

2 Cut along all horizontal, vertical and diagonal lines, then open out and press the resulting bi-coloured squares. If necessary unpick the stitches across the corners. You will have eight bi-coloured squares from each original pair.

3 Using four bi-coloured squares for each, stitch two pinwheels in each of the five colours (diagram 2).

diagram 2

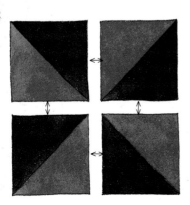

4 To make the additional green/black pinwheels, place the black and medium green rectangles, right sides together and mark out six squares instead of four. Use the resulting 12 bi-coloured squares to make three pinwheels following steps 1 to 3.

5 Make a template from the tracing paper 3½ in/9 cm square. Using flat headed pins, pin this template to one of the pinwheels, tilting the paper so that the corners touch the edges of the pinwheel (diagram 3).

diagram 3

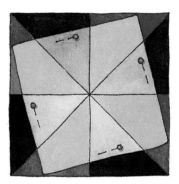

6 Cut around the paper to skew the pinwheel and produce the windmill blocks. The diagonal seams will be displaced from the corners. In each pair of colours tilt the paper one way, then the other to vary the effect (diagram 4).

diagram 4

7 Lay out the yellow, mauve and green strips in sequence, following the quilt assembly diagram on page 74. Working from the lefthand side of the quilt top, cut the first yellow strip across the width about halfway down. Stitch a green and black windmill block to one of the cut edges, taking a ¼ in/0.75 cm seam allowance. Press the seam towards the strip, then place the second half of the yellow strip on the opposite edge of the windmill block and stitch as before. Press the seam towards the strip.

8 Next, cutting the strips randomly to vary the position of the pinwheels, repeat with the remaining strips.

9 Stitch the strips together in sequence. Press the seams, then trim the top and the bottom edges of the quilt to make them straight.

FINISHING

1 Layer the quilt top with the backing and wadding, then baste the three layers together in a 4 in/10 cm grid.

2 Using invisible thread, quilt down the vertical seams "in the ditch", then, using the variegated thread, quilt in random zig zags, first down each strip, then adding another zig zag line in between these strips (diagram 5).

diagram 5

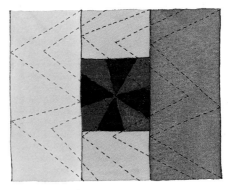

3 Trim the wadding and backing level with the quilt top. From the remaining green fabric, cut strips 2½ in/6 cm wide to a total length of 175 in/445 cm. Use double-folded to bind the edges with straight binding strips.

Scrap Triangles

This double bed quilt has an all over design of triangles made from a multitude of scraps. The basic unit is a square made of half triangles in dark/medium values of printed fabrics. Constructed in blocks of sixteen and 24 units, each block has two or three smaller triangle units made in a bright/dark combination to add focus points across the quilt. These are positioned randomly to add to the effect of spontaneity. The size can easily be changed by making more or fewer units. To make this size, eight of the blocks need extra units i.e. 4 x 6 instead of 4 x 4. The design is completed on a longarm quilting machine.

MATERIALS

All fabrics used in the quilt top are 45 in/115 cm wide, 100% cotton

Patterned fabric scraps in dark and medium values:
11 yards/11 metres in total, for the larger triangles – any pieces 4 in/10 cm or larger can be used
Patterned fabric scraps in brights and dark values:
2¼ yards /2.25 metres in total, for the smaller triangles – any pieces 2½ in/6.5 cm or larger can be used
Backing: 94 x 100 in/239 x 254 cm
Wadding: 2 oz or low loft, 94 in x 100 in/239 x 254 cm
Binding: patterned cotton, ¾ yard/75 cm
Variegated blue machine quilting thread

Quilt size: 90 x 96 in/229 x 244 cm

Quilt assembly diagram

CUTTING

● **Dark and medium patterned scraps**, begin by cutting 40 x 4 in/10 cm squares of each, to make the large triangle units.

● **Bright and dark patterned scraps**, begin by cutting 20 x 2⅜ in/6 cm squares of each, to make the small triangle units.

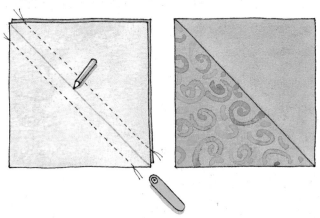

Note:
As you work more of the large and small units can be cut and stitched to supplement those you have. This way of working will keep up the interest as you make the quilt, rather than cutting every square you will need before starting to stitch.

STITCHING

1 To make the large triangle units, place a medium and a dark 4 in/10 cm square right sides together, then draw one diagonal line from corner to corner and stitch ¼ in/0.75 cm away from this diagonal line on either side. Cut along the line, open out and press. Trim the resulting bi-coloured squares to exactly 3½ in/9 cm. Make sure that the seam line still runs corner to corner (diagram 1). Repeat to use up the 80 squares cut.

diagram 1

2 To make the small triangle units, place two pairs of the bright and dark 2⅜ in/6 cm squares right sides together and follow the same procedure as for the larger triangle described in step 1. Stitch the four resulting bi-coloured squares together to make the smaller triangle units (diagram 2). Repeat to use up the 40 squares cut.

diagram 2

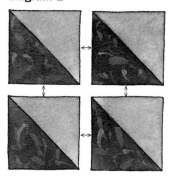

3 Although this is essentially an all-over design with no distinct divisions, the units are stitched together in blocks for ease of handling. When you have prepared an adequate number of large and small triangle units, lay them on a flat surface in sets of sixteen. Most of the blocks in this quilt have 14 of the large triangle units and two of the smaller ones. Just a few have three of the smaller ones. Position the smaller units randomly as you construct the blocks. As you stitch the units together be sure to place all the dark fabrics on the same side of the diagonal divisions (diagram 3).

diagram 3

4 Cut more squares and repeat steps 1 and 2 to make a total of 840 of the large triangle units and 120 of the smaller ones. Continue to lay them out in blocks as described in step 3. You will need a total of 48 blocks of 16 units and 8 blocks of 24 units (see quilt assembly diagram).

5 When you have completed all the blocks, stitch them together, first into sets of twelve or sixteen. Finally stitch these together, keeping to the correct sequence. This will avoid many long seams.

FINISHING

1 If you plan to do your own quilting, spread the backing right side down on a flat surface, then smooth the wadding and the quilt top, right side up on top. Pin, then stitch horizontal and vertical grid lines of basting about 4 in/10 cm apart.

> Note:
> When working with a large quilt this procedure is much easier if you work with a helper to keep the three layers smooth and flat.

2 Using the "free motion machine quilting" method and referring to the picture as a guide, quilt over the surface of the quilt in variegated blue machine quilting thread. Alternatively, use a longarm quilting machine. The quilt pictured here was quilted by Beryl Cadman of "Custom Quilting" using her own interpretative freehand style.

3 Trim the backing and wadding level with the edges of the quilt and bind the edges with a double-fold binding cut 2½ in/6 cm wide, mitring the corners.

Dancing Pinwheels

This wallhanging or bed quilt is made with a combination of two blocks using mostly hand-dyed fabrics. The "Crazy Log Cabin" blocks are quickly constructed in sets of eight and these form the background for the tilted pinwheel blocks which are made in high contrast bright/dark or light/dark combinations to create focus points. Minimal measuring and marking make this a quick and easy project for the beginner. The finished size can easily be altered by making more or fewer blocks. You could also impose your own interpretation on the basic design idea by altering the positions of the pinwheels or making more or fewer of them in relation to the crazy blocks. A longarm quilting machine was used to finish the design.

MATERIALS

All fabrics used in the quilt top are 45 in/115 cm wide, 100% cotton

For the "crazy log cabin" blocks: a total amount of 4 yards/4 metres or 16 fat quarters (one fat quarter will yield four squares; sixty-two are required altogether)
For the pinwheels: scraps of bright/dark fabrics to a total of 1 yard/1 metre
Wadding: 2 oz or low loft, 64 x 64 in/162 x 162 cm
Binding: cotton, ½ yard/50 cm
Tracing paper: one A4 sheet
Backing: cotton, 64 x 64 in/162 x 162 cm
Flat-headed flower pins
Multicoloured machine quilting thread

Quilt size: 60 x 60 in/152 x 152 cm

Quilt assembly diagram

CUTTING

● **For the "crazy log cabin" blocks,** cut 7 sets of 8 x 8½ in/22 cm squares of differently coloured fabrics, keeping them in separate piles; cut 1 more set of 6 x 8½ in/22 cm squares of differently coloured fabrics (62 squares in total)

● **For the pinwheels,** cut 19 x 3¾ in/9.5 cm squares in bright or light colours; 19 x 3¾ in/9.5 cm squares in dark colours; 19 x 3⅜ in/8.5 cm squares in bright or light colours; 19 x 3⅜ in/8.5 cm squares in dark colours.

STITCHING

1 The "crazy log cabin" blocks are constructed in multiples of eight at a time. To make the first set, take one of the sets of eight cut squares and make sure they are stacked with right sides uppermost, then press with a steam iron to make them cling together.

2 Place the fabrics on your cutting board and, using the diagram 1a as a guide and a rotary cutter, cut all layers together into six pieces. Cut freely and, as you do so, visualize the pieces in their finished size (i.e. without their seam allowance). It may help to turn the cutting board a quarter turn for each cut. Move the sets of pieces slightly away from each other but keep them together in the cutting pattern until they are required for stitching (diagram 1b).

diagram 1a

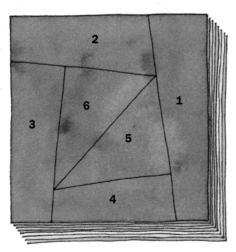

diagram 1b

3 Spread all the centre right pieces (i.e. no. 5) out on a flat surface, then take the centre left pieces (no. 6) and place right sides together with a no. 5 piece in a different fabric. Stitch the pairs together using a scant seam allowance to make the centre piece. Press the seams to one side (diagram 2).

diagram 2

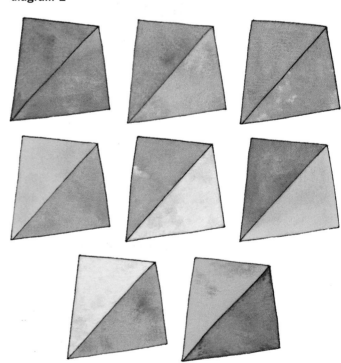

4 Stitch the strips to the centre pieces in the reverse order of cutting, i.e. 4, 3, 2, then 1, mixing the fabrics as you work (diagrams 3 a to d). Make sure that you stitch the first strip (no. 4) to the correct side of the centre square. There are six pieces in each block, so working with eight squares, you can avoid colour

diagram 3a

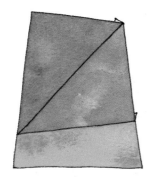

diagram 3b

diagram 3c

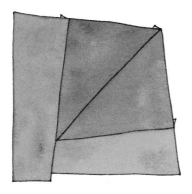

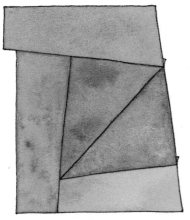

diagram 3d

5 Cut a 6½ in/16.5 cm square of tracing paper. Using the flat-headed pins, pin the paper to each block in turn and trim away the outer edges with your rotary cutter. The flat-headed pins will allow the rotary ruler to lie flat over the fabrics as you cut (diagram 4).

diagram 4

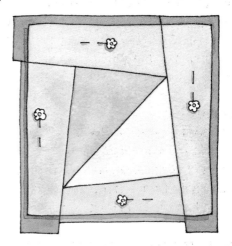

6 Repeat steps 1 to 5 to make another six sets of blocks with eight fabrics and the final set with six to make sixty-two blocks altogether. Each time you cut a set of blocks you may like to vary the cutting pattern slightly to give each set a slightly different appearance (diagram 5).

diagram 5

 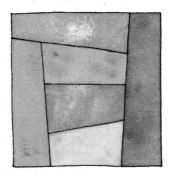

repeats in any one block. When all the strips are stitched you will have eight blocks with uneven edges. Where two edges to be stitched together are of slightly different lengths, align the edges at the broadest end of the strip to maximize the size of the block.

7 To make each tilted pinwheel block, you will need three different fabrics plus additional scraps for the borders. Select two 3¾ in/9.5 cm squares which have a high contrast, e.g. a light/dark or bright/dark combination. Place these right sides together, then mark two diagonal lines across from opposite corners on the wrong side of the lighter square. Stitch from the centre to the edges, ¼ in/0.75 cm from the diagonal lines (diagram 6). Cut across both diagonals to make four bi-coloured triangles.

diagram 6

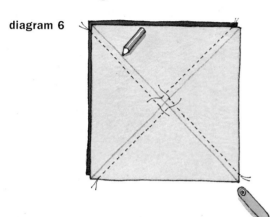

8 Take two 3⅜ in/8.5 cm squares of the third fabric choice and divide these across one diagonal to make four corner triangles. Stitch one pieced triangle to one corner triangle four times, then stitch the resulting squares first in pairs, then the pairs together to make the pinwheels (diagram 7).

diagram 7

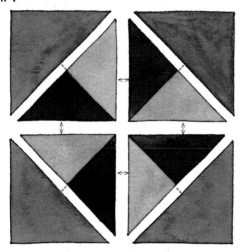

9 Using short lengths of scrap fabric, stitch a 1¾ in/4.5 cm border to all four sides of the pinwheel in log cabin sequence (diagram 8).

diagram 8

10 Next, using the same square paper template that you used to cut out the crazy log cabin blocks, pin this to the pinwheel block at a skewed angle, so that the corners of the paper touch the edges of the block and cut out (diagram 9).

diagram 9

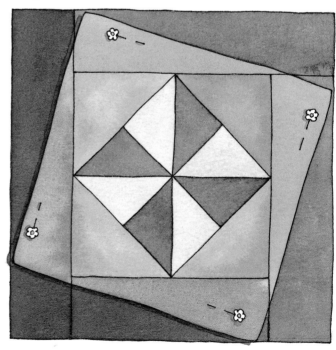

11 Repeat steps 7 to 10 to make nineteen pinwheel blocks in total. The paper template can be tilted in either direction to vary the design (diagram 10).

diagram 10

12 Arrange all the blocks on a vertical design wall or large flat surface, distributing the pinwheels across the surface and scattering or grouping the colours in the crazy blocks to make a pleasing composition.

13 Stitch all blocks together, first in rows, then the rows together. Press.

FINISHING

1 If you plan to do your own quilting, lay out the backing, wadding and pieced top and fasten together with safety pins or baste in a grid.

2 Using the "free motion machine quilting" method and referring to the photograph as a guide, quilt over the surface of the quilt in multicoloured machine quilting thread. The quilt pictured here was quilted by Beryl Cadman of "Custom Quilting" on a longarm quilting machine using her own freehand style.

3 Trim the backing and wadding level with the edges of the quilt. Cut strips 2½ in/6 cm wide from the binding fabric and use to bind the edges with a double-fold binding, mitred at the corners.

SOFT AND WARM

Anne Walker

All the quilts in this chapter are made in brushed flannels, either printed or woven. The designs have been kept simple, as brushed fabrics are naturally softer and more flexible, so do not lend themselves to designs that involve intricate piecing. Flannel quilts are wonderful to snuggle under on chilly evenings. To retain the softness of the quilts, they should not be over-quilted. All the designs in this chapter could equally successfully be interpreted in ordinary cotton cloth.

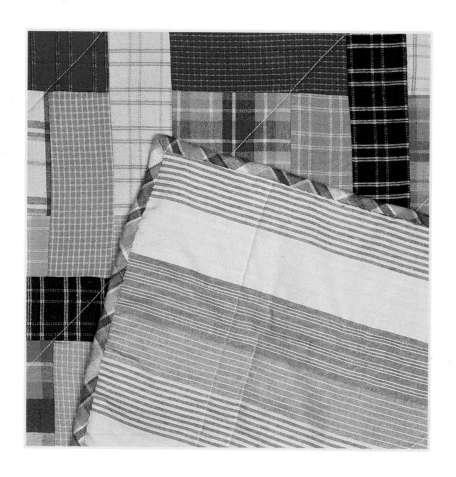

Plaid Pavement

This simple design is a great way to showcase a range of fabric colours or patterns. In the quilt shown I have used a very bright set of flannel plaids that are available in large and small scale weaves.

MATERIALS

All fabrics used are 45 in/115 cm wide

Assorted large-scale plaids for block centres and binding: 12 fat quarters in total
Assorted small-scale plaids for blocks and the outer borders: 12 fat quarters in total
Dark fabric for inner border and corner squares: ⅝ yard/50 cm
Wadding: lightweight, 60 x 76 in/155 x 195 cm
Backing: 4⅜ yards/4 metres for a lengthwise join or 3⅜ yards/3 metres for a crosswise join

Quilt size: 58 x 74 in/150 x 190 cm

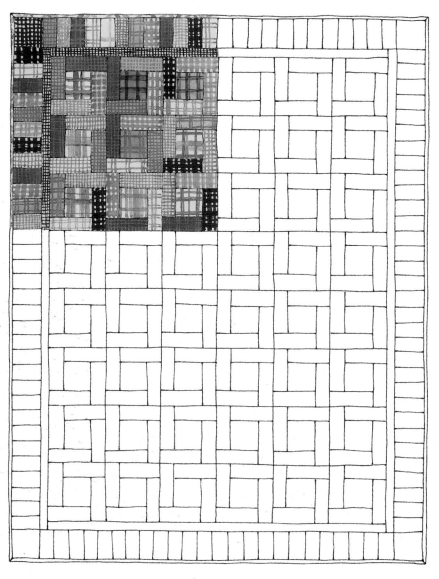

Quilt assembly diagram

ALTERNATIVE COLOURWAYS

Top left: soft coloured plaid and striped flannels for those cooler evenings in spring; top right: choose a print fabric for your centre square and select coordinating fabrics to surround it; bottom left: a Christmas motif surrounded by holly fabrics makes a good colour scheme for a festive quilt: choosing just two fabrics for the strips and placing them on adjacent sides will give a trellis design to the quilt when the blocks are placed side by side; bottom right: a basket of sunflowers forms the block centre - again two fabrics are selected for the strips but this time when the blocks are placed side by side a double width basket-weave design appears.

CUTTING

- **Large-scale plaids**, from each design cut 4 squares, 4½ x 4½ in/ 11.5 x 11.5 cm
- **Small-scale plaids**, from each design cut 16 rectangles, 2½ x 6½ in/6.5 x 16.5 cm; from the remainder, cut rectangles, 2½ x 4½ in/6.5 x 11.5 cm for outer border
- **Dark fabric**, cut 6 strips, 1½ in/3.5 cm wide for inner border and 4 squares, 4½ x 4½ in/11.5 x 11.5 cm

STITCHING

You will make 48 blocks each using an assortment of 5 different plaids. The method of construction is the same for all the blocks.
Stitch all seams using an accurate ¼ in/0.75 cm seam allowance.

1 Select a large plaid square for the centre of the block and four 2½ x 6½ in/6.5 x 16.5 cm rectangles to surround it.

2 Stitch rectangle 1 to the righthand edge of the square, stitching only three-quarters of the seam (diagram 1). Press the seam towards the rectangle.

diagram 1

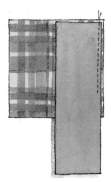

3 Rotate the block and stitch rectangle 2 to the edge of the centre square and across the end of rectangle 1 (diagram 2). Press the seam towards the added rectangle.

diagram 2

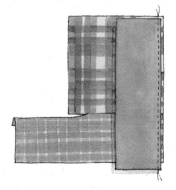

4 Rotate the block and stitch rectangle 3 to the edge of the centre square and across the end of rectangle 2 (diagram 3). Press the seam towards the added rectangle.

diagram 3

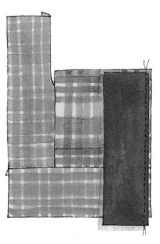

5 Rotate the block and stitch rectangle 4 to the edge of the centre square and across the end of rectangle 3 (diagram 4). Press the seam towards the added rectangle.

diagram 4

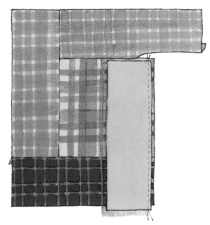

6 Complete the seam that joins rectangle 1 to the centre square and across the end of rectangle 4. Press the seam towards rectangle 1. You now have a completed block (diagram 5). Repeat to make a total of 48 blocks.

diagram 5

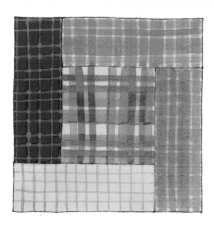

7 Following the quilt assembly diagram on page 90, lay the blocks out in a 6 x 8 grid. Try to avoid the having fabrics of the same design next to each other. When you are pleased with the layout, stitch the blocks in rows. Press the seams of each row in alternate directions.

8 Stitch the rows together, then press all the seams in one direction.

ADDING THE BORDERS

1 Join the six strips of dark inner border fabric.

2 Measure across the centre of the quilt. Using this measurement cut two pieces from the border fabric. Stitch to the top and bottom of the quilt. Press the seams towards the borders.

3 Measure the length of the quilt down the centre, including the added borders. Using this measurement cut two pieces from the remaining border fabric. Stitch to the sides of the quilt. Press the seams towards the borders.

4 Using the small-scale plaid rectangles, mix the designs in a random fashion and stitch two border strips each with 26 rectangles and two border strips each with 34 rectangles. Press all the seams in one direction.

5 Stitch a long strip to each side of the quilt. Press the seams towards the inner borders.

6 Stitch a square of dark fabric onto each end of the short borders. Press the seams towards the squares. Stitch these borders to the top and bottom of the quilt, pressing the seams towards the inner borders.

FINISHING

1 Lay out the backing, wadding and pieced top and fasten together with safety pins or baste in a grid. Quilt in a design of your choice. I machine quilted in a diagonal grid through the corners of the blocks.

2 Cut 2½ in/6.5 cm wide bias strips from the remaining large plaid fabrics. Join these randomly into one long strip and use to bind the quilt with a double-fold binding, mitred at the corners.

Friendship Plaids

This lap quilt mixes woven plaids with printed flannels, together with the odd piece of cotton fabric, to great effect. The whole quilt is quick and easy to make and the top could be pieced in just a day.

MATERIALS

All fabrics in this quilt are 45 in/115 cm wide, but a working measurement of 40 in/100 cm is assumed as some fabrics when brushed come up slightly narrower

Assorted plaids and flannels: 10 fat quarters, including lights, mediums and darks for the blocks
Plain, light cotton: 1 fat quarter
Inner border, dark cotton: ⅜ yard/30 cm
Outer border and backing, floral: 3¼ yards/3 metres
Binding, dark cotton: ⅝ yard/50 cm
Wadding: lightweight, 50 x 62 in/130 x 155 cm

Quilt size: 46 x 58 in/120 x 145 cm

Quilt assembly diagram

CUTTING

● **Plaids and flannels:** from each of the **10 fat quarters,** cut 3 squares, 6½ x 6½ in/16.5 x 16.5 cm; cut 3 strips, 2½ in/6.5 cm, sub-cut these strips into squares, 2½ in/6.5 cm.

● **Plain, light cotton,** cut 48 squares, 2½ x 2½ in/ 6.5 x 6.5 cm.

● **Inner border fabric,** cut 4 strips, 2½ in/6.5 cm.

● **Outer border/backing fabric,** cut the fabric in half and piece into a rectangle, 60 x 90 in/150 x 225 cm, from this cut a rectangle, 50 x 60 in/125 x 150 cm; from remainder cut 4 strips, 6½ x 60 in/16.5 x 150 cm.

● **Binding fabric,** cut 9 strips, 2½ in/6.5 cm.

STITCHING

There are three blocks used in this quilt (see diagram 1). The large squares for Block A (6½ x 6½ in/16.5 x 16.5 cm) are already cut.

diagram 1

**Block A
make 25**

**Block B
make 5**

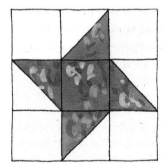

**Block C
make 9**

1 To make the nine-patch block, Block B, lay out nine assorted 2½ in/6.5 cm squares. Referring to diagram 2, join the squares in rows. Join the rows to make up the block. Make five blocks in total.

diagram 2

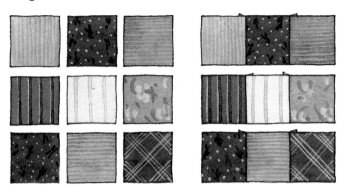

2 There are two types of Block C, the friendship star block. Of the nine blocks in total, four of the blocks are for the corners and have plain light backgrounds; the remaining five are for the main body of the quilt and can have backgrounds of your choice. For each star, choose one background fabric and one star fabric from your 2½ in/6.5 cm squares. For each block you will use five star squares and eight background squares.

3 To make the star points, pair together four star squares and four background squares. Place them right sides together and draw a line across the diagonal of the lightest fabric. Stitch on this line. You may chain piece if you wish (diagram 3).

diagram 3

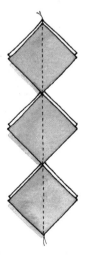

4 Place the ¼ in/0.75 cm line of your ruler on the stitched line of each pair and trim away (diagram 4). These small waste triangles can be saved for another project. Press the stitched triangle units towards the darkest fabric.

diagram 4

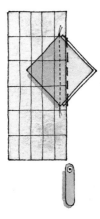

5 Lay out the squares for a block and stitch the squares into rows, pressing towards the squares and away from the pieced units. Stitch the rows together to make the blocks (diagram 5). Set aside the four corner blocks.

diagram 5

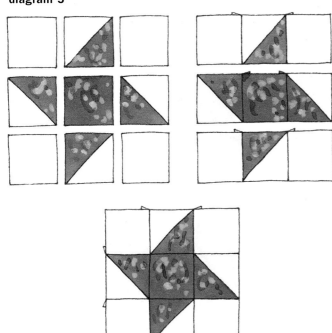

6 Following the quilt assembly diagram on page 94, lay out the blocks for the centre of the quilt. Try to mix the fabrics as much as possible. Join the blocks into rows. Press the seams in the rows in alternate directions. Join the rows together to make the top, matching seams where necessary. Press all the seams in one direction.

ADDING THE BORDERS

1 Measure the top across the centre from side to side. Cut two inner border strips to this length and stitch to the top and bottom of the quilt. Press towards the borders.

2 Measure through the centre of the quilt from top to bottom, including the added borders. Cut two inner borders to this length and stitch to the sides of the quilt. Press towards the added borders.

3 Measure the pieced top across the centre and down the middle. Using these two measurements cut four outer border strips to these lengths, two short and two long. Stitch the two long strips to the sides of the quilt and press towards the added borders.

4 Stitch a corner friendship star block to each end of the short strips and press towards the border strip. Stitch these borders to top and bottom of the quilt. Press outwards.

FINISHING

1 Sandwich the quilt top, wadding and backing together and pin or baste in a grid.

2 Quilt in a design of your choice, either by hand or with a longarm quilting machine.

3 To complete the quilt, join the binding strips and bind with double-fold binding, mitring the corners.

Hidden Stars

This soft-coloured flannel quilt makes a great table-cloth or could be made as a cosy lap quilt. The "easy corners" method is used to construct the blocks to speed up the process. All the triangles that are cut away during the piecing can be saved for another project when speed is not a consideration.

MATERIALS
All fabrics in this quilt are 45 in/115 cm wide printed flannels, but a working measurement of 40 in/100 cm is assumed as some fabrics when brushed come up slightly narrower

Gold background and border: 2¾ yards/2.5 metres
Dark blue: 2¾ yards/2.5 metres
Dark red: 1⅝ yards/1.5 metres
Binding (red): ⅝ yard/50 cm
Backing: 3¼ yards/3 metres for a lengthwise join, 3⅞ yards/3.5 metres for a crosswise join
Wadding: lightweight, 56 x 72 in/140 x 180 cm

Quilt size: 52 x 68 in/130 x 170 cm

Quilt assembly diagram

CUTTING

● **Gold**, cut 5 strips, 8½ in/21.5 cm wide, from these strips cut 17 squares, 8½ x 8½ in/21.5 x 21.5 cm and 6 rectangles, 4½ x 8½ in/11.5 x 21.5 cm; cut 5 strips, 4½ in/11.5 cm wide, from these strips cut 18 rectangles, 4½ x 8½in/11.5 x 21.5 cm; cut 4 squares 4½ x 4½ in/11.5 x 11.5 cm; cut 8 strips, 2½ in/6.5 cm wide for the borders.
● **Dark blue**, cut 5 strips, 8½ in/21.5 cm wide, from these strips cut 18 squares, 8½ x 8½ in/21.5 x 21.5 cm; cut 12 strips, 4½ in/11.5 cm wide, from these strips cut 96 squares, 4½ x 4½ in/11.5 x 11.5 cm.
● **Dark red**, cut 12 strips, 4½ in/11.5 cm wide, from these cut 96 squares, 4½ x 4½ in/11.5 x 11.5 cm.
● **Red binding**, cut 8 strips 2½ in/6.5 cm wide.
● **Backing**, cut into 2 pieces and join to make a rectangle, cut from this a backing measuring 56 x 72 in/ 140 x 180 cm.

STITCHING

All seams are an accurate ¼ in/0.75 cm.

There are two different "square in a square" blocks for the body of the quilt, one made from the two dark fabrics and one made from the gold fabric combined with the dark blue fabric (diagram 1). Both blocks are constructed the same way.

diagram 1

Block A
make 17   **Block B**
make 18

1 To make Block A, take 68 small squares of the dark blue fabric and, on the wrong side, draw a line across one diagonal.

2 Place a marked square of dark blue fabric on the corner of a large square of gold fabric, right sides together (diagram 2). Stitch along the drawn line. Repeat 17 times. You can chain piece the blocks if you wish.

diagram 2

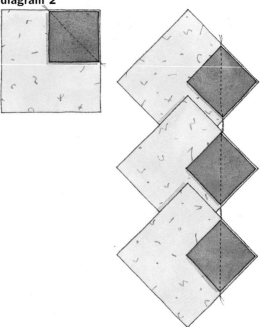

3 Repeat the process for the opposite corner of the large square (diagram 3). Cut apart.

diagram 3

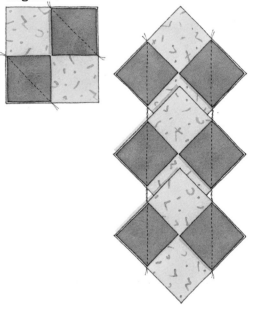

4 Place the ¼ in/0.75 cm line of your ruler on the stitching line of each block and cut away the unwanted triangles. Repeat for both sides of the square and press seams towards the triangle (diagram 4).

5 Repeat this "easy corner" technique for the other two corners of the square until you have 17 blocks.

6 To make Block B, use 18 large dark blue squares and 72 small squares of dark red fabric. Make 18 blocks using the "easy corner" technique as for Block A.

diagram 4

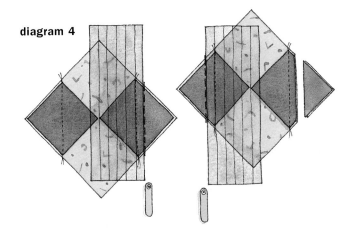

7 Next make the border blocks. Again, there are two different blocks, each made in the same way (diagram 5). To make Block C, take the remaining small squares of dark red fabric and draw a diagonal line on the wrong side as shown in diagram 2. Place a square right sides together with a rectangle of gold background fabric and stitch on the drawn line (diagram 6). Chain piece if liked.

diagram 5

Block C
make 10

Block D
make 14

diagram 6

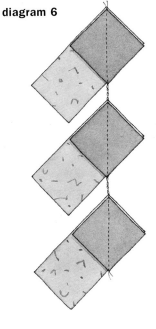

8 Cut the pieces apart. Place the ¼ in/0.75 cm line of your ruler on the stitching line and cut away the unwanted triangles. Press towards the triangle (diagram 7).

9 Repeat the "easy corner" technique for the other side of the rectangle (diagram 8). Trim and press as before. Repeat until you have 10 border blocks.

10 To make Block D repeat as for block C, using the remaining gold background rectangles and the small dark blue squares. Make 14 blocks in total.

diagram 7   **diagram 8**

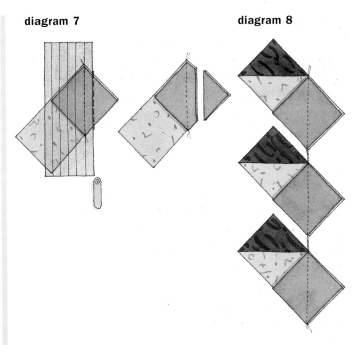

11 Lay out the blocks as shown in the quilt assembly diagram on page 98. Include the border blocks and the four small gold background squares to complete the design. Piece each row horizontally. Press odd rows to the left and even rows to the right. Stitch the rows together matching the seams where appropriate. Press all the seams one way.

ADDING THE BORDERS

1 Using the border strips, stitch together in pairs to make four long strips. Press the seams open.

2 Measure across the centre of your quilt top from side to side. Cut two of the long border strips to this length and stitch to the top and bottom of the quilt. Press towards the borders.

3 Measure the quilt top through the centre from top to bottom, including the borders, and cut the remaining long strips to this length. Stitch to the sides of the quilt and press towards the borders.

FINISHING

1 Layer the quilt top, wadding and backing. Pin or baste in a grid from the centre out.

2 Quilt in a pattern of your choice. I have machine quilted in diagonal lines following the outline of the stars.

3 Join the binding strips and bind the quilt with a double-fold binding, mitring the corners.

Steps to the Stars

This cosy quilt is easy to make in time for those chilly winter evenings. The larger the variety of reds and greens that you can use, the better. In the quilt featured I have used thirteen different reds and ten greens.

MATERIALS

All fabrics used are 45 in/115 cm wide, brushed cotton

Solid black for centre squares: ½ yard/40 cm
Assorted red homespuns: 1⅜ yards/120 cm in total
Assorted green homespuns: 1⅜ yards/120 cm in total
Gold homespun for stars: ⅜ yard/30 cm
Fusible web: 1⅛ yards/1 metre
Wadding: lightweight, 51 x 51 in/130 x 130 cm
Backing: 51 x 51 in/130 x 130 cm

Quilt size: 47 x 47 in/120 x 120 cm

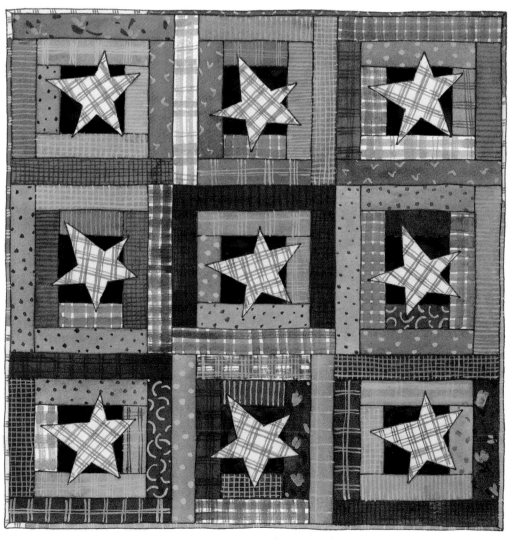

Quilt assembly diagram

CUTTING

Cut all strips across the fabric from selvage to selvage.

● **Black fabric**, cut 2 strips 6 in/16.5 cm wide; from these strips cut 9 squares measuring 6 x 6 in/ 16.5 x 16.5 cm.

● **Red fabrics**, cut 15 strips each 3 in/8.5 cm wide; from these strips randomly cut the following rectangles: 8 pieces, 3 x 6 in/8.5 x 16.5 cm; 18 pieces, 3 x 11 in/8.5 x 30.5 cm; 10 pieces, 3 x 16 in/8.5 x 44.5 cm.

● **Green fabrics**, cut 15 strips each 3 in/8.5 cm wide; from these strips randomly cut the following rectangles: 10 pieces, 3 x 6 in/8.5 x 16.5 cm; 18 pieces, 3 x 11in/8.5 x 30.5 cm; 8 pieces, 3 x 16 in/8.5 x 44.5 cm.

● **Gold fabric**, using the template on page 105, trace 9 star shapes onto the paper side of the fusible web. Cut round these stars leaving a small margin. Iron each of these star shapes on to the wrong side of the gold fabric. Cut out exactly on the traced lines. Set aside for later.

STITCHING

All seams are stitched with an accurate ¼ in/0.75 cm seam allowance.

Refer to diagram 1 for placement of logs for the blocks used in this quilt.

1 With piece A as a black square, stitch green rectangles (3 x 6 in/8.5 x 16.5 cm) in positions B and C. Press towards these green strips. Now add green rectangles (3 x 11 in/8.5 x 30.5 cm) in positions D and E. Press towards these green strips. Add red rectangles (3 x 11 in/8.5 x 30.5 cm) in positions F and G. Press towards these red strips. Finally, add red rectangles (3 x 16 in/8.5 x 44.5 cm) in positions H and I. Press towards these red strips. This completes Block A. Make five blocks in total.

2 To make Block B, follow instructions as for Block A (step 1), but substitute red rectangles in the place of green and green rectangles in the place of red. Make four blocks in total.

diagram 1

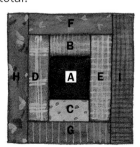

3 Lay out the blocks as shown in diagram 2. Rearrange the positions if necessary to spread the fabric selection as randomly as possible. Join the blocks in three rows of three. Press the seams open. Join the three rows together. Press the seams open.

diagram 2

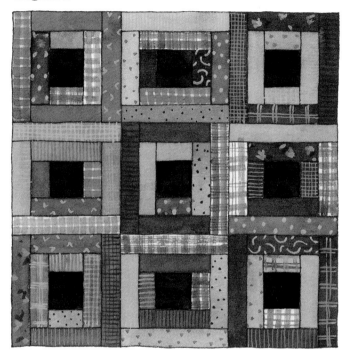

4 Taking the nine stars that you have already prepared, peel off the backing paper and fuse one star to the centre of each block, altering the direction of the stars as you go. Using either a blanket stitch on your sewing machine or by hand, stitch round each of the stars.

FINISHING

1 Sandwich the top, wadding and backing and pin together or baste in a grid. Quilt as you wish, either by hand or using a longarm quilting machine.

2 Trim the wadding and backing to the size of the quilt top. Using the remaining pieces from the strips for the blocks, cut the strips down to 2¼ in/6.5 cm wide. Join end to end until you have a length of binding measuring approximately 200 in/500 cm. Press for double-fold binding and use to bind the edges of the quilt.

template

Ohio Star Medallion

This simple flannel quilt makes a cosy throw. It is shown here in soft, muted colours, but it would look good in any colour scheme. It is a good quilt in which to use up some of those odd "fat quarters" that you may have left over from other projects.

MATERIALS

All fabrics used in the quilt top are 45 in/115 cm wide, woven or printed flannels

Assorted fabrics: 14 fat quarters
Light stripe for background of 4 of the blocks and light squares of the corner nine-patches:
½ yard/50 cm
Large check for first border: 1 fat quarter
Second large check for third border: ⅞ yard/75 cm
Wadding: lightweight, 64 x 64 in/160 x 160 cm
Backing: 64 x 64 in/160 x 160 cm
Binding: leftover scraps to make a pieced binding or leftover backing fabric

Quilt size: 60 x 60 in/150 x 150 cm

Quilt assembly diagram

CUTTING

● **For the nine-patch blocks (make 4 sets):**

light stripe fabric, cut 4 squares, 4½ x 4½ in/11.5 x 11.5 cm;

assorted fabrics, cut 5 squares, 4½ x 4½ in/11.5 x 11.5 cm.

● **For the Ohio star blocks (make 13 sets):**

from the background fabric, cut 4 light squares, 4½ x 4½ in/ 11.5 x 11.5 cm;

cut 1 square, 5¼ x 5¼ in/12.5 x 12.5 cm, and sub-cut twice on the diagonal to give 4 triangles;

from the assorted fabrics, for the centre square A: cut 1 square, 4½ x 4½ in/11.5 x 11.5 cm;

for the accent triangles B: cut 1 square, 5¼ x 5¼ in/ 12.5 x 12.5 cm, and sub-cut twice on the diagonal to give 4 triangles;

for the star points C, cut 2 squares, 5¼ x 5¼ in/ 12.5 x 12.5cm, and sub-cut twice on the diagonal to give 8 triangles.

● **For the first border:**

large check fabric, cut 4 strips, 12½ x 4½ in/31.5 x 11.5 cm;

dark fabric, cut 4 squares, 4½ x 4½ in/11.5 x 11.5 cm.

● **For the second border:**

assorted fabrics, cut 24 squares, 4½ x 4½ in/11.5 x 11.5 cm.

● **For the third border:**

second large check fabric, cut 4 rectangles, 28½ x 4½ in/ 71.5 x 11.5 cm;

dark fabric, cut 4 squares, 4½ x 4½ in/11.5 x 11.5 cm.

STITCHING

1 For the nine-patch blocks, take four light squares, and five assorted dark squares. Referring to diagram 1, lay out the squares and stitch them into rows. Stitch the rows into blocks. Press all the seams towards the dark fabrics. Make four blocks in total.

diagram 1

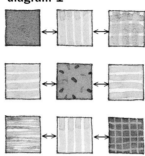

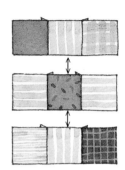

2 For the Ohio star blocks, lay out the pieces as shown in diagram 2. To make the 4-triangle unit, stitch the triangles in pairs and press towards the star point fabric. Stitch these larger triangles to form a square, which should measure 4½ in/11.5 cm (diagram 3).

3 Lay out the block as in diagram 4, stitch the squares into rows, pressing towards the blank square, and stitch the rows together to complete. Make 13 blocks in total.

diagram 2

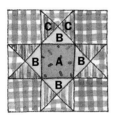

diagram 3

diagram 4

4 Following the quilt assembly diagram on page 106, construct the quilt from the centre. Choose one of the star blocks for the centre.

ADDING THE BORDERS

1 For the first border, stitch a 12½ in/31.5 cm strip of the large check fabric to the top and bottom of the centre star. Press towards the added strip. Stitch a 4½ in/11.5 cm dark square to both ends of the

diagram 5

remaining two large check strips. Press towards the squares. Stitch one of these to each side of the centre star. Press towards the added strips (diagram 5).

2 For the second border, stitch two strips of five squares and stitch these to the top and bottom of the centre unit. Now stitch two strips of seven squares and stitch to each side of the centre unit. Press towards the added borders.

3 For the third border, stitch two of the rectangles to the top and bottom of the centre unit. Press towards the added borders. Stitch a square on each end of the remaining rectangles, pressing towards the squares, and stitch these to the sides of the centre unit. Press towards the added borders (diagram 6).

diagram 6

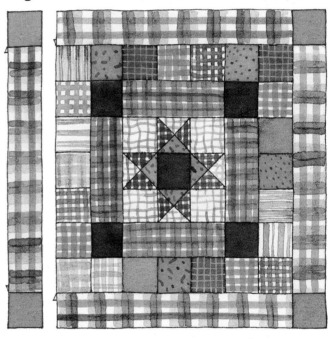

4 For the final border, refer to the quilt assembly diagram on page 106. Place the four stars with the light stripe background in the middle of each side. Join the three stars for the top edge and stitch to the centre. Join the three stars for the bottom edge and stitch to the centre. Finally, join the three stars for either side, stitch a nine patch to each end of these units and stitch to the sides.

FINISHING

1 Sandwich the quilt layers together and pin or baste in a grid. Quilt as desired, either by hand or machine.

2 Make up 2¼ in/6.5 cm double-fold binding from any of your remaining backing fabric or from your scraps and use to bind the quilt, mitring the corners.

COUNTRY FLOWERS

Rebecca Collins

Flowers are a popular source of inspiration for many things and for many people. Whether it is their delicate fragrance that fills a room; their colours in a vase; their shapes added to wallpaper, decorator fabrics or indeed furniture, they are an important part of our lives. We often use flowers in interior decor to bring a feeling of the peace and open air of the country to our living rooms. The quilts in this section have taken the theme of flowers, either in their actual design or in the fabric choice, to encapsulate that country-fresh feeling. Make them using similar fabrics or choose ones that will reflect your personal preference and room decoration.

Log Cabin Flowers

Ideal as a throw, this quilt is quick and easy to make, using chain piecing, Big Stitch and "stitch in the ditch" quilting techniques. "Log cabin" blocks are a popular patchwork design. Off-centre log cabin blocks create a curved look when joined together, and the addition of a 3D unit at the centre of four of these blocks gives the illusion of a flower.

MATERIALS

All fabrics used in this quilt top are 45 in/115 cm wide, 100% cotton

Flower fabrics: 2¾ yards/2.5 metres
Leaf/Background fabrics (green): 1¼ yards/1.25 metres
Flower centres and inner border fabrics (pink): ½ yard/50 cm
Outer border and binding: no piecing seams in border: 2½ yards/2.25 metres; with piecing seams: 2 yards/1.75 metres
Backing: 65 x 82 in/165 x 205 cm
Wadding: 2 oz, 65 x 82 in/165 x 205 cm
Threads: Perlé no. 8 to match/contrast flower fabric and leaf/background fabric; Tanné 30 for the "stitch in the ditch" quilting

Quilt size: 60½ x 77 in/153 x 195 cm

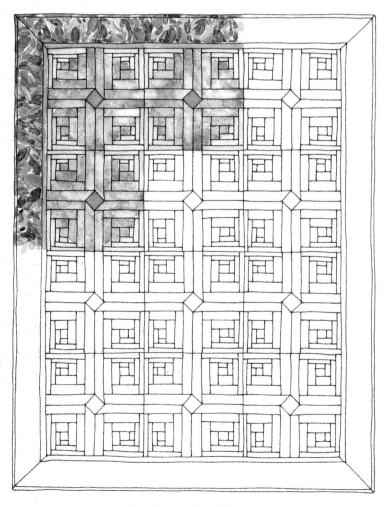

Quilt assembly diagram

ALTERNATIVE COLOURWAYS

Top left: a sunflower effect is achieved by the use of yellow and brown for this block; top right: a monochromatic colourway in this combination creates a softer look; bottom left: be dramatic - choose a dark background/leaf fabric and one of the bolder colours within it for the flower; bottom right: the use of the vibrant plaid for this flower makes a bright and cheerful statement.

CUTTING

- **Flower fabrics,** 42 medium strips, 2 in/5.25 cm wide.
- **Leaf/Background fabrics,** 33 narrow strips, 1¼ in/ 3.25 cm wide.
- **Flower centres,** 12 squares, 3½ in/9 cm.
- **Inner border,** 6 strips, 1½ in/4 cm wide.
- **Outer border,** cutting the strips either across the fabric and joined or parallel with the selvage for no joins, 2 strips, 4¾ x 77 in/12 x 195 cm, and 2 strips 4¾ x 50 in/12 x 127 cm. Reserve the remainder for the binding.

STITCHING

All seam allowances are the usual ¼ in/0.75 cm.

1 Place one flower fabric medium strip and one leaf/background fabric narrow strip right sides together and stitch along one long edge. Press seam towards the narrow strip. Cross-cut this strip at 2 in/5.25 cm intervals (diagram 1). Make 48 of these units.

2 Place one of these two-piece units at the top edge of a narrow green strip, right sides together, aligning the raw edges (see diagram 2). Stitch the unit to the strip, stopping just before reaching the end of the unit with the needle down in the fabric. Pick up another unit and place it on the strip just below the unit just stitched. Continue stitching the first unit to the strip and onto the second unit. Continue chain piecing in this way until you have filled the strip with the two-piece units. Repeat until all the two-piece units have been stitched to a narrow strip.

diagram 1   **diagram 2**

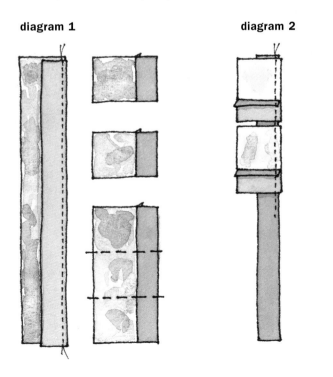

3 Cross-cut the narrow strips between each of the two-piece units. You now have three-piece units. Press seam towards the strip just added (diagram 3).

4 With the strip just added at the bottom, place a three-piece unit on the top edge of a medium flower strip, right sides together. Align the raw edges and stitch together (diagram 4). Chain piece as before and continue until the strip is full of units. Repeat until all the three-piece units have been added to a medium strip.

diagram 3   **diagram 4**

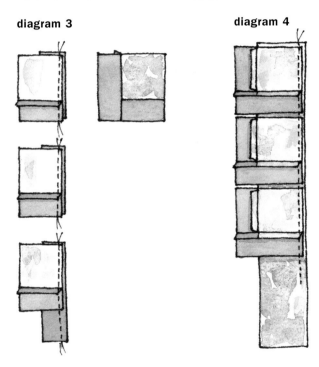

5 Cross-cut the medium strips between each of the three-piece units. You now have four-piece units. Press the seam towards the strip just added.

6 Repeat steps 4 and 5 with another medium strip and the four-piece units. Remember to place the units onto the medium strip with the last strip added at the bottom.

7 Now add a narrow strip to the five-piece units. Remember that the last strip added is always placed at the bottom when being stitched to the next strip. Cut apart and press as before. Add a second narrow strip, cut apart and press as before. Then repeat the procedure with two medium strips. Continue in this manner, adding two narrow, then two medium strips, until you have a block with three narrow strips and three medium strips around a centre square. This is one completed off-centre log cabin block (diagram 5). Make 48 blocks in total.

diagram 5

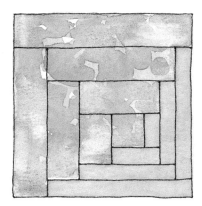

8 Take a pink flower centre and fold in half with wrong sides together. Place a block right side up on a table with the medium strips in the upper righthand corner. Place the folded square in the top righthand corner of this block with the long raw edge to the top, aligning all raw edges. Pin to secure (diagram 6).

diagram 6

9 With right sides together, place a second block on top of the first block, aligning all raw edges and ensuring that the medium strips of both blocks are aligned with each other. Stitch together along the righthand edge, thus catching the short edge of the folded square (diagram 7).

diagram 7

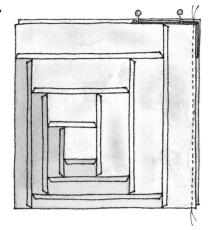

10 Open out the unit just stitched and fold the two blocks back until the wrong sides touch each other and the folded square extends to the right.

11 Place another block right side up on the table with the medium strip corner in the top right. Position the unit created in step 10 on top of this block with the folded strip in the top right corner, aligning all raw edges. Secure with pins (diagram 8).

diagram 8

12 Place another block right sides together on top of this unit. Ensuring that the corners containing the medium strips on both blocks are matching and that all raw edges are aligned. Stitch these together along the edge containing the short end of the folded strip.

13 Open out the unit. You will now have the folded square held in place at each end by a pair of blocks (diagram 9).

diagram 9

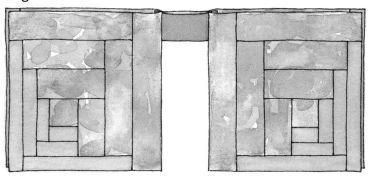

14 Open out the pairs of blocks and align the centre seams joining the two blocks. Make sure the two seam allowances are pressed in opposite directions. Secure with a pin either side of this junction. Gently pull out the fabric of the folded square as far as it will go (it will extend 1½ in/4 cm from the seam). Take care that only the raw edges of this fabric are going to be caught in the seam. Secure with pins. Repeat on the other side of the centre seam with the fabric of the folded square. Secure with pins. Align all raw edges of the blocks and the centre square and stitch together along the top edge (diagram 10).

diagram 10

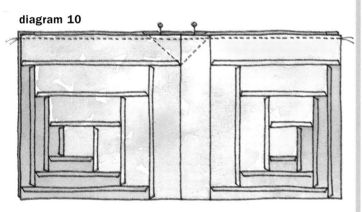

15 Open out the unit. You now have four blocks stitched together with a 3D centre – a Log Cabin Flower. Press the seams taking care not to put a strong crease on the fold of the 3D centre. Make twelve "flowers" in total.

16 Following the quilt assembly diagram on page 112, stitch four "flowers" together to form a vertical row. Make three rows. Either press the seams in alternate directions on each row or press them open. Stitch these three rows together to form a group of three rows, each containing four flowers. Press the seams open.

ADDING THE BORDERS

1 Measure the width of the top and bottom edges of the quilt. Stitch the inner border strips together and from this cut two strips to this measurement. Stitch to the top and bottom edges of the quilt.

2 Measure the length of the sides of the quilt and cut two strips to this measurement. Stitch the strips to the sides of the quilt.

3 Stitch the shorter outer border strips to the top and bottom of the quilt. Stitch the longer outer border strips to the sides of the quilt.

FINISHING

> Note:
> Depending on the fabric, you may find it easier to make a template for the quilting designs rather than tracing them onto the quilt top.

1 Mark the top ready for quilting. If using templates the marking can be done as and when needed. Sandwich the quilt top together with the backing and wadding. Baste or pin the three layers together.

2 I have used "in-the-ditch" quilting around each "flower" and around both edges of the inner border, using Tanné 30 thread on the top and an ordinary thread in the bobbin. "Triple straight stitch" was used. This is a "utility stitch" which can be found on most modern sewing machines. Then I used Big Stitch hand quilting and perlé no. 8 to stitch the quilting motifs opposite in the strips. The outer border has straight line quilting running from the quilt out to the edge.

3 Use the remaining outer border fabric to create the bias binding strips 2½ in/6.5 cm wide. Stitch the binding to the quilt prior to trimming away the excess wadding and backing. This excess helps to stabilize the work while binding is being machined into position.

*Left: Quilting motif for the narrow strips –
align registration marks with the seam where the
four blocks come together*

*Below: Quilting motif for the medium strips –
align the centre square with the 3D fabric centres*

Anemones Wall Hanging

This wall hanging is made using a very easy method of raw edge appliqué for the petals of the flowers. The raw edge helps to give the flowers a softer and perhaps a more realistic look, and because the raw edges are on circles rather than on straight edges there is little or no fraying. The flower centres are textured, then embellished with beads and added embroidery. A simple trellis surrounds the anemones within the wall hanging. If anemones do not appeal, try using the same techniques to create poppies in their many colours.

MATERIALS

All fabrics used in this wall hanging are 45 in/115 cm wide, 100% cotton

Background (soft yellow): 1½ yards/1.5 metres
Trellis (brown or woodgrain print): ½ yard/50 cm
5 flower colours (reds and blues): ¼ yard/25 cm of each colour
White: ¼ yard/25 cm
Black: ¼ yard/25 cm
Border (plaid): 1¼ yards/1.25 metres
Backing: 47 in/117.5 cm square plus 6 x 45 in/ 15 x 115 cm for sleeve
Wadding: 2 oz, 47 in/117.5 cm square
Small beads
Black embroidery thread
Black quilting thread plus colours of your choice
Small embroidery hoop

Quilt size: 43 in/107.5 cm square

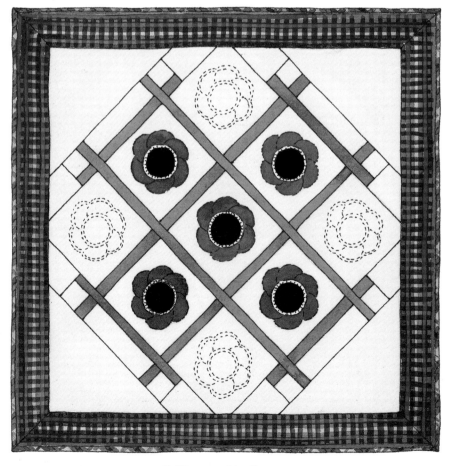

Quilt assembly diagram

CUTTING

- **Background yellow fabric**, 2 strips, 8½ in/21.5 cm, cut these into 9 squares, 8½ in/21.5 cm;
1 strip, 14 in/35 cm, cut this into 2 squares, 14 in/35 cm, cut each square on the diagonal into two triangles;
2 strips, 3½ in/9 cm, cut these into 8 pieces, 3½ x 6½ in/9 x 16.5 cm;
2 strips, 2½ in/6.5 cm, cut 1 of these strips into 4 lengths, 8½ in/21.5 cm.
- **Trellis brown fabric**, 1 strip, 1½ in/4 cm wide;
2 strips, 1½ x 31½ in/4 x 79 cm;
2 strips, 1½ x 14½ in/4 x 36.5 cm;
8 strips, 1½ x 8½ in/4 x 21.5 cm.
- **Flower fabrics**, using the small circle template below right, 6 circles of each colour, 3¼ in/8.25 cm in diameter.
- **White fabric:** 5 small circles.
- **Black fabric:** using the large circle template below left, 5 circles, 4 in/10 cm in diameter.
- **Border plaid fabric:** 4 strips, 4 in/10 cm. Reserve the remainder for the binding.

STITCHING

1 Take a 8½ in/21.5 cm square of background fabric and mark the centre. Place six small circles of the same colour in the centre of the square, each overlapping the other and equally spaced. All the circles will just meet in the middle. Secure with pins (diagram 1).

diagram 1

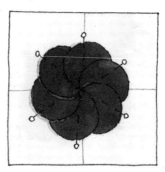

diagram 2

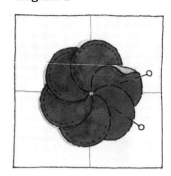

2 Stitch around the edge of each circle, ¼ in/0.75 cm from the edge, starting near the middle where the circles just touch. There is no need to stitch on the areas that will eventually be covered by the white circle. When nearing the edge of the next circle lift it so that the stitching can continue underneath for about ½ in/1.25 cm. On the last circle, stitch up to the stitching line on the first circle (diagram 2).

3 Once all stitching has been completed, place a white circle in the centre and secure with pins.

4 Take a black circle and stitch a long gathering stitch ¼ in/0.75 cm from the edge all round.

5 Gather up the black circle slightly. Place it on top of the white circle, pinning it temporarily in the centre with one pin. Remove the pins from the white circle underneath. Continue pulling up the threads until the edge of the black circle is ¼ in/0.75 cm from the edge of the white circle. Secure with pins (diagram 3).

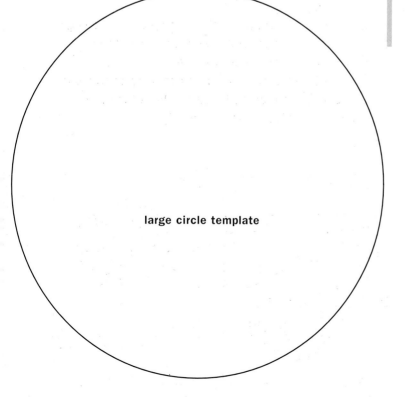

large circle template

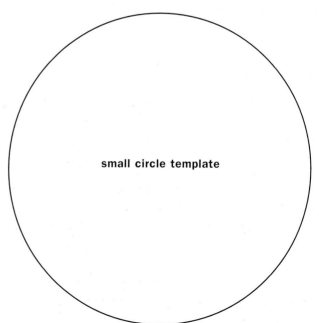

small circle template

6 Stitch the black circle to the centre of the "flower", stitching on top of the gathering stitches.

7 Turn the square over and cut away the background fabric and the "petal" fabric within the stitched centre circle, allowing a ¼ in/0.75 cm seam allowance on the inside of the stitching. This will remove the excess bulk created by the overlapping fabrics. Take care not to cut through the white or black fabric (diagram 4).

diagram 3   **diagram 4**

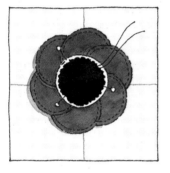 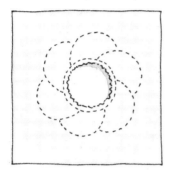

8 Place the square in an embroidery hoop. Using a strong matching thread, such as quilting thread, knot the thread, then push the needle up through the black fabric to the front. Make a small stitch in the same place catching the black fabric to the white circle underneath.

9 In exactly the same place, push the needle through to the back. Now bring the needle out to the front in another position. Again, catch the black fabric down to the white circle underneath. Repeat these stitches, placing them randomly over the surface of the black circle, until the surface "puckers" are as dense as you like.

10 Stitch beads randomly across the surface among the folds, then using embroidery thread, stitch a combination of a straight stitch with a French knot at one end around the edge of the black circle, overlapping the white circle and just touching the flower petals.

11 Make up all five flowers as described above.

12 Place the 1½ x 45 in/4 x 115 cm trellis strip on top of a 2½ x 45 in/6.5 x 115 cm strip of background fabric, right sides together. Press the seam towards the trellis fabric. Cross-cut into eight 2½ in/6.5 cm units.

13 Stitch an 8½ in/21.5 cm trellis strip to the top and bottom edge of three of the flower squares. Press the seams towards the trellis fabric.

14 Stitch a 8½ in/21.5 cm square of background fabric to the top and bottom edge of two of these squares. Press the seams towards the trellis fabric.

15 Stitch a 8½ in/21.5 cm trellis strip to the top edge of one flower square and the bottom edge of the remaining flower square, then stitch one of the 8½ x 2½ in/21.5 x 6.5 cm pieces of background fabric to the trellis strip on each square. Press the seams towards the trellis fabric (diagram 5).

diagram 5

16 Take two 8½ x 2½ in/21.5 x 6.5 cm background strips and stitch one of the units cut in step 12 to both ends of each strip, ensuring that the trellis fabric strip is sandwiched in between the background fabric. Press the seams towards the trellis fabric (diagram 6).

17 Stitch a 14½ in/36.5 cm trellis strip to the right edge of one of these strips and to the left edge of the other. Press the seam towards the trellis fabric (diagram 7).

diagram 6   **diagram 7**

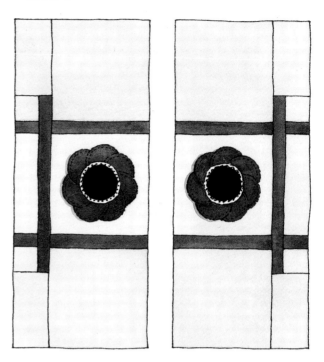

diagram 8

18 Stitch a 3½ x 6½ in/9 x 16.5 cm background piece to both ends of each of the units just created. Press the seams towards the piece just added.

19 Stitch the units created in step 18 to the units created in step 14, taking care to put the sides with the vertical trellis strips next to the squares containing the flowers. Align so that the short section of horizontal trellis fabric matches the trellis above and below the flower. Press the seams towards the trellis fabric (diagram 8).

20 Fold one of these units so that the trellis above and below the flower are one on top of the other. Mark the position of the fold. Fold one of the large triangles to find the centre of the long edge. With right sides together, align these two centre marks. Pin the remaining portion of the triangle into position and stitch together. The long strip will extend beyond the triangle at this stage. Repeat with the second unit (diagram 9).

diagram 9

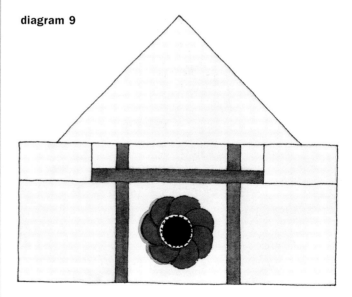

21 Stitch a unit made in step 12 to one end of four 3½ x 6½ in/9 x 16.5 cm pieces of background fabric. Stitch one of the resulting units onto the plain squares at each end of the units created in step 20, taking care over positioning (diagram 10).

diagram 10

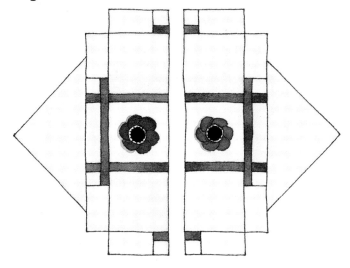

22 Stitch the two flower units with the trellis only on the top or bottom edge to the remaining flower unit. Then stitch the 31½ in/79 cm trellis strips to either side of this unit (diagram 11).

diagram 11

23 Stitch the units completed in step 21 to either side of this three-flower unit and then add a triangle to each end as in step 20. Place the pieced unit on the cutting board. Align a ruler with the edges of the large triangles and cut off those portions that extend beyond the edge of the ruler. Measure the completed item to ensure that it is square (diagram 12).

diagram 12

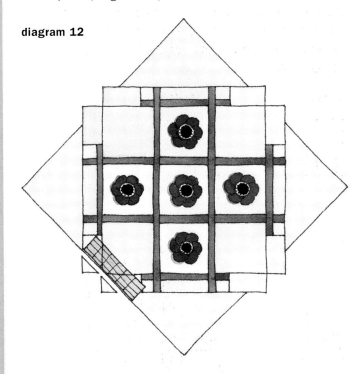

ADDING THE BORDERS

1 Stitch a border strip to each side of the completed top making either abutted corners or mitred corners, as liked.

FINISHING

1 Sandwich the wall hanging top with the wadding and backing. Quilt anemone motifs in the plain squares, following the quilt assembly diagram on page 118. Stitch "in the ditch" around the trellis and at the edge of the border. Add straight quilting lines over the whole top except for the flowers and trellis and finally add two straight lines of quilting in the border.

2 Use the remaining border fabric to create the bias or straight strips for the binding and apply to the hanging. Finally, add the hanging sleeve.

Sweet Pea Reversible Quilt

This reversible quilt is created with a combination of the "quilt-as-you-go" technique, a different backing fabric for each of the two blocks, and joining-strips that become a part of the overall design. The only part of the quilt that is done by hand is the "finishing" of the joining-strips and binding. Sweet pea fabric has been used on both sides of this quilt but you could have two totally different colour schemes if you prefer.

MATERIALS

All fabrics used in this quilt are 45in/115 cm wide, 100% cotton

Sweet pea fabric: 10½ yards/9.5 metres
Green contrast fabric: 2¼ yards/2 metres
Red fabric: 2½ yards/2.25 metres
Peach fabric: 2¼ yards/2 metres
Yellow fabric: 3¼ yards/3 metres
Wadding: 2 oz, 1 kingsize packet or 4½ yards/ 4.25 metres, 60 in/150 cm wide

Quilt size: 96 in/240 cm square

Quilt assembly diagram (front)

CUTTING

● Sweet pea fabric:

Top and bottom borders: (diagram 1)
Cut off a 75½ in/189 cm piece. Remove the selvages. Cutting parallel with the selvage, cut:
2 strips, 10 in/26 cm (label these "top and bottom borders back");
2 strips, 9 in/24 cm (label these "top and bottom borders front");
2 strips, 1½ in/4 cm (label these "top and bottom joining-strips").

Side borders: (similar to diagram 1 but longer piece)
Cut off a 95½ in/239 cm piece. Remove the selvages. Cutting parallel with the selvage, cut:
2 strips, 10 in/26 cm (label these "side borders back");
2 strips, 9 in/24 cm (label these "side borders front");
2 strips, 1½ in/4 cm (label these "side joining-strips").

Joining-strips/Block backs/Borders: (diagram 2)
Cut off a 62½ in/156.5 cm piece. Remove the selvages. Cutting parallel with the selvage, cut:
4 strips, 1½ in/4 cm (label these "vertical joining-strips");
Cutting across the width of the fabric, cut:
2 strips, 13 in/32.5 cm, from each of these cut 2 squares, 13 in/32.5, and 8 strips, 1½ in/4 cm;
1 strip, 13 in/32.5 cm, from this cut 2 squares, 13 in/32.5 cm, 4 strips, 1½ in/4 cm, 2 strips widthways, 6½ in/16.5 cm, from one of these cut 4 strips, 1½ in/4 cm;
1 strip, 13 in/32.5 cm, from this cut 2 squares, 13 in/32.5 cm, and 2 squares, 6½ in/16.5 cm;
4 squares, 7 in/17.5 cm, cut each square in half on the diagonal (label these "small inner border triangles").
(label all the 13 in/32.5 cm squares "block backs", all the 6½ in/16.5 cm squares "corner squares" and all the 1½ x 13 in/4 x 32.5 cm strips "horizontal joining-strips).

diagram 1

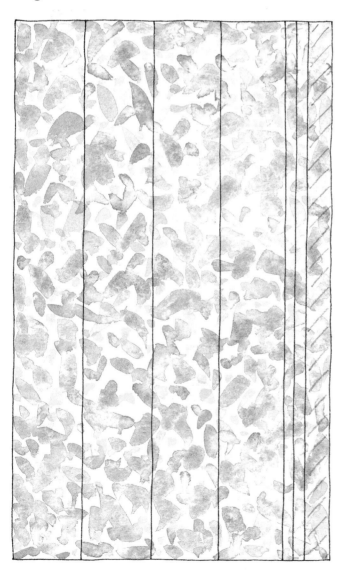

diagram 2

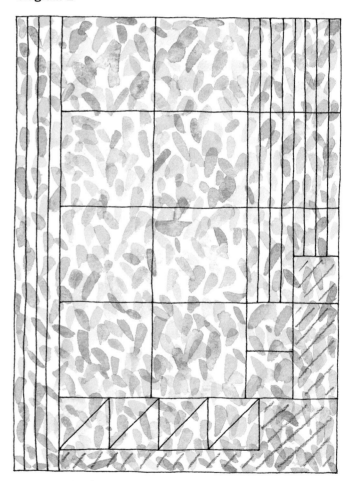

diagram 3

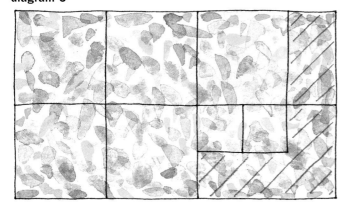

Block backs/Corner squares: (diagram 3)
Cutting across the fabric, cut:
1 strip, 13 in/32.5 cm, from this cut 3 squares,
13 in/32.5 cm ("block backs");
1 strip, 13 in/32.5 cm, from this cut 2 squares,
13 in/32.5 cm ("block backs"), and 2 squares,
6½ in/16.5 cm ("corner squares").
Nine-patch strips:
Cutting across the fabric, cut:
7 strips, 4½ in/11.5 cm.

diagram 4

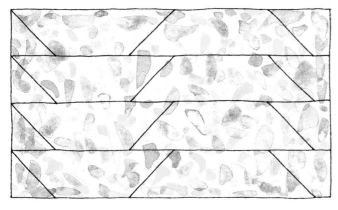

Border Pieces: (diagram 4)
Cutting across the fabric, cut:
4 strips, 6½ in/16.5 cm, from these use the template on
page 131 enlarged to full size to cut 8 border pieces.
● **Green contrast fabric:**
Cutting across the width of the fabric, cut:
4 strips, 13 in/32.5 cm, from these cut 12 squares,
13 in/32.5 cm;
1 strip, 13¼ in/33.5 cm, cut this into 3 squares,
13¼ in/33.5 cm, cut each of these squares into 4
triangles on each diagonal.
● **Red fabric:**
Remove selvages and cut:
2 strips, 1 x 75½ in/2.75 x 189 cm (label these "side
joining-strips");

6 strips, 1 x 62½ in/2.75 x 156.5 cm (label these
"top/bottom and vertical joining-strips");
20 strips, 1 x 12½ in/2.75 x 31.5 cm (label these
"horizontal joining-strips");
4 strips, 1 x 6½ in/2.75 x 16.5 cm (label these "corner
joining-strips on border").
● **Peach fabric:** 5 strips, 4½ in/11.5 cm;
2 strips, 13½ in/34 cm, from these cut 6 squares,
13½ in/34 cm;
1 strip, 13¼ in/33.5 cm, cut this into 3 squares, 13¼ in/
33.5 cm, cut each square into 4 triangles on each diagonal.
● **Yellow fabric:** 1 strip, 7 in/17.5 cm, from this cut
4 squares, cut each square in half on the diagonal
(label these "small inner border triangles");
1 strip, 6½ in/16.5 cm, from this cut 4 squares (label
these "corner squares");
4 strips, 6½ in/16.5 cm, from these cut 8 border
pieces using the template (diagram 4);
3 strips, 4½ in/11.25 cm;
2 strips, 13½ in/34 cm, from these cut 6 squares,
13½ in/34 cm;
1 strip, 13¼ in/33.5 cm, cut this into 3 squares, 13¼ in/
33.5 cm, cut each square into 4 triangles on each diagonal.
● **Wadding:** 2 strips, 10 x 96 in/26 x 240 cm;
2 strips, 10 x 76 in/26 x 190 cm;
2 strips, 7 x 76 in/17.5 x 190 cm;
4 strips, 7 x 63 in/17.5 x 157.5 cm;
25 squares, 13 in/32.5 cm;
4 squares, 7 in/17.5 cm.

STITCHING

All seam allowances are the usual ¼ in/0.75 cm.

1 To make the nine-patch blocks, stitch a 4½ in/11.5 cm strip of peach fabric to either side of a 4½ in/11.5 cm strip of sweet pea fabric. Press seams towards the sweet pea fabric. Make two of these units. Cross-cut these three-strip units at 4½ in/11.5 cm intervals (diagram 5a).

2 Stitch a 4½ in/11.5 cm strip of sweet pea fabric to either side of a 4½ in/11.5 cm strip of yellow fabric. Press seams towards the sweet pea fabric. Cross-cut this three-strip unit at 4½ in/11.5 cm intervals (diagram 5b).

3 Stitch one of the units created in step 1 to either side of a unit created in step 2. Press the seams open. Make nine of these nine-patch blocks in total (diagram 5c).

4 Repeat steps 1 to 3, but this time use two yellow strips with one of the sweet pea fabric and one peach strip with two strips of sweet pea fabric. Make one three-strip unit of each colour combination. Make four of these nine-patch blocks in total (diagram 5d).

diagram 5a   **diagram 5b**

diagram 5c   **diagram 5d**

5 Place a sweet pea fabric block back wrong side up on the table. Place a 13 in/32.5 cm square of wadding on top of this square. Place a nine-patch block right side up on top of the wadding. The backing and wadding will be slightly larger than the pieced block. Pin or baste in position. Do this with all thirteen nine-patch blocks.

6 Place a 13½ in/34 cm yellow square on top of a 13½ in/ 34 cm peach square, right sides together. On one of the squares draw a diagonal line from corner to corner. Stitch the two squares together ¼ in/0.75 cm either side of the drawn line. Cut apart on the drawn line. Open out and press the seam towards one of the triangles (diagram 6).

diagram 6

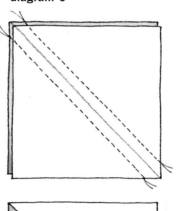

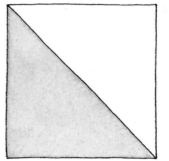

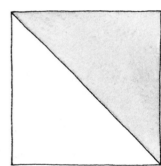

7 Place one of the two-triangle squares right side up with the yellow triangle in the top right corner. Place a second two-triangle square on top, right sides together, with the peach triangle in the top right corner. Draw a diagonal line from the top right corner to the lower left corner. Stitch these two squares together and cut apart as before. You now have two squares each containing four triangles. Make twelve of these units in total (diagram 7).

diagram 7

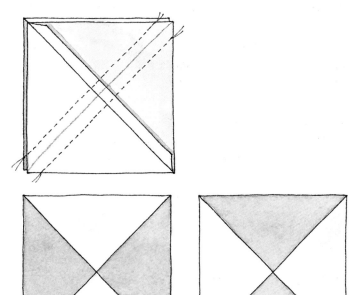

8 "Sandwich" each of the units created in step 7 together with 13 in/32.5 cm squares of wadding and the 13 in/32.5 cm squares of green fabric.

9 Machine quilt the nine-patch and four-triangle blocks with a standard straight stitch following the patterns in diagram 8. Trim each block to 12½ in/31.5 cm square.

diagram 8

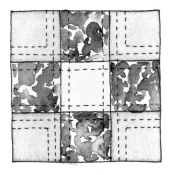

10 To join the blocks, fold the horizontal sweet pea joining-strips in half lengthwise, wrong sides together, and press. Trim these strips to 12½ in/31.5 cm.

11 Take a nine-patch block with yellow centre square and place on the table with pieced side face down. Pin a horizontal red joining-strip along one edge with right sides together aligning all raw edges.

12 Turn the block over. Along the edge where the red strip has been pinned, pin a folded sweet pea fabric strip matching ends and raw edges. Secure with pins. Stitch these together (diagram 9). Fold the red strip on the back up and away from the block and finger press.

diagram 9

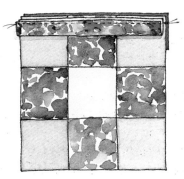

13 Take a four-triangle block and place on the table with one of the peach triangles at the top but with the green backing square uppermost. Now place the nine-patch block created in step 12 over this block, with the red joining-strip at the top and right sides together with the green backing square, aligning all raw edges. Pin and stitch the red joining-strip to the block (diagram 10).

diagram 10

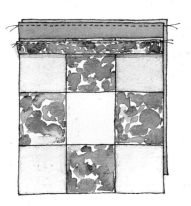

14 Open out the unit just created. Fold the sweet pea joining-strip over to hide the seams. Stitch this folded edge in position by hand. Two reversible blocks have now been joined (diagram 11).

diagram 11

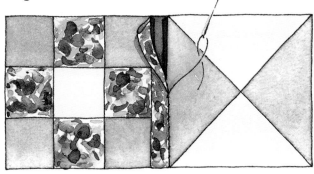

15 Following the quilt assembly diagram for the front of the quilt on page 124 and taking great care over block placement, join the blocks together as descibed above in vertical rows.

16 Use the four 62½ in/156.5 cm vertical joining-strips to join the rows together in exactly the same way as the blocks. Take care to align all the horizontal joining-strips.

ADDING THE BORDERS

1 Following diagram 12, piece the borders using the peach/green triangles, the yellow/sweet pea segments cut using the template (enlarged to the correct size), and the yellow/sweet pea small inner border triangles. These triangles will be slightly large. Trim to size after piecing the border. Make four of these border units in each colour grouping (peach and yellow/green and sweet pea).

diagram 12

2 Sandwich one border unit of each fabric combination with a strip of wadding of the same size. Be sure to align all seams. Secure with pins or basting. Following diagram 13, machine quilt all four of the border units using the standard straight stitch.

diagram 13

3 Using the remaining top and bottom joining-strips in sweet pea and red, trimmed if necessary, stitch a border unit to the top and bottom edge of the central section (diagram 14).

diagram 14

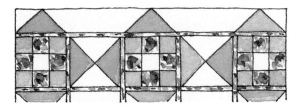

4 Sandwich together 6½ in/16.5 cm squares of sweet pea fabric/wadding/yellow fabric. Make four of these units. Using the 6½ in/16.5 cm joining-strips, join these to each end of the two remaining border units (diagram 15).

diagram 15

5 Join these border units to the sides of the quilt using the side joining-strips in sweet pea and red, trimmed as necessary, taking care to align the horizontal joining-strips.

6 Place a 9 in/24 cm sweet pea top border front strip right sides together on the "front" (the pieced block side) of the quilt along the top edge, aligning raw edges. Pin in place. Place a 10 in/26 cm sweet pea top border back strip right sides together on the "back" of the quilt and along the same edge, aligning all raw edges. Again, pin in place. Stitch these border strips to the quilt (diagram 16).

diagram 16

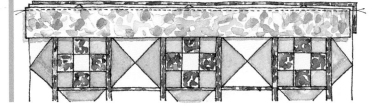

7 Fold the border strip on the back up and away from the quilt. Place a piece of wadding of the correct size on top of this border strip. By hand, lightly stitch the edge of the wadding to the seam allowance.

8 Fold the "front" border strip up onto the wadding. It will not quite cover the wadding. Pin or baste the three layers together (diagram 17).

diagram 17

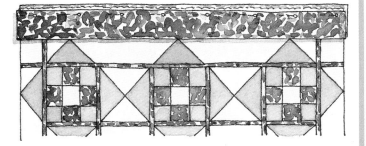

9 Repeat steps 6 to 8 using bottom border strips to add the border at the bottom edge of the quilt.

10 Now, using the same procedure and side border strips, add the side borders to the quilt.

FINISHING

1 Quilt the outer border, following the pattern in diagram 18.

diagram 18

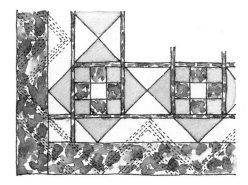

2 Use the remaining sweet pea fabric to create bias strips for the binding, 2½ in/6.5 cm wide. Apply a double-fold binding to the quilt, mitring the corners.

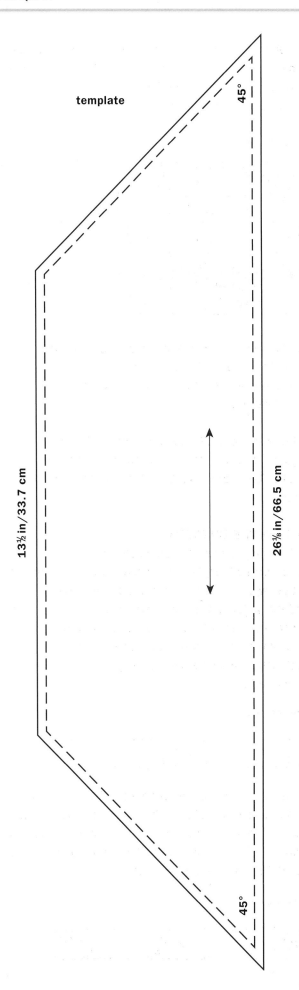

template

45°

13½ in/33.7 cm

26⅞ in/66.5 cm

45°

Forget-me-not Dreams

With quick piecing methods and production line assembly this bed quilt can be made very quickly. The simple pieced flowers in two scales will give any bedroom a fresh country feel. Choose the colour of your favourite flower or a colour to suit your décor. I have also made a matching pillowcase. I worked out the design on graph paper first based on a finished case size of 20 x 30 in/50 x 75 cm with a 3 in/7.5 cm wide edging. To make this you need an extra 1¾ yards/1.75 metres background fabric plus 30 x 40 in/75 x 100 cm each of wadding and backing. The flowers and border can be made from the left-overs from the quilt.

MATERIALS

All fabrics used in the quilt are 45 in/115 cm wide, 100% cotton

Background (white patterned): 5 yards/4.75 metres
Green: 3½ yards/3.25 metres
Blue: 1 yard/1 metre
Yellow: ¼ yard/25 cm
Wadding: 2 oz, 99 x 74 in/251 x 188 cm
Backing: 99 x 74 in/251 x 188 cm

Quilt size: 95 x 70 in/241 x 178 cm

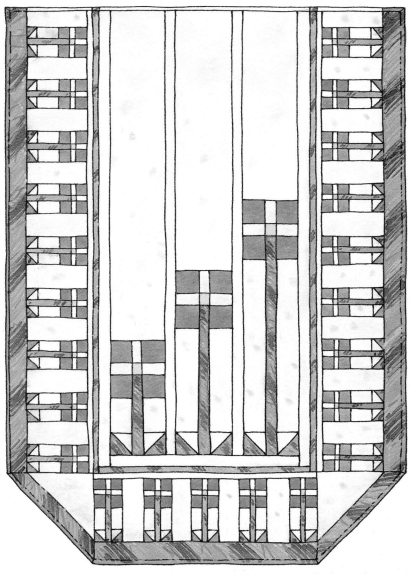

Quilt assembly diagram

CUTTING

● **Background fabric:** (diagram 1)

Cut a piece 84 in/210 cm long and remove the selvages. Cutting parallel to the selvage, cut:

1 strip, 10½ in/26.5 cm wide; from this cut 1 strip (C) 57½ in/144 cm, 2 pieces (D) 4½ x 18½ in/11.5 x 46.5 cm;

1 strip, 10½ in/26.5 cm wide; from this cut 1 strip (E) 45½ in/113.75 cm, 2 pieces (F) 4½ x 30½ in/11.5 x 76.5 cm, 2 pieces (G) 4½ x 6½ in/11.5 x 16.5 cm;

1 strip, 10½ in/26.5 cm wide; from this cut 1 strip (H) 38½ in/96.5 cm, 1 strip (I) 1½ x 40½ in/4 x 101.5 cm, 1 strip (J) 2½ x 40½ in/6.5 x 101.5 cm, 3 squares (K) 4⅞ in/12.5 cm, 3 strips (L) 2½ x 4½ in/6.5 x 11 cm;

4 strips (A) 2½ in/6.5 cm;

2 strips (B) 1½ in/4 cm.

> **Note:**
> If you are unable to cut the last 1½ in/4 cm wide strip cutting parallel to the selvage, cut two strips 1½ in/4 cm across the width of the fabric and piece these together to form one long strip. When required cut this to the correct length.

From remaining background fabric (diagram 2) and cutting across the width of the fabric, cut:

1 strip (M) 2½ in/6.5 cm;

3 strips (N) 4½ in/11.5 cm;

3 strips (O) 1½ in/4 cm;

3 strips, 11½ in/29 cm, cross-cut these into 22 rectangles (P) 4½ in/11.5 cm wide;

2 strips, 2⅞ in/7.5 cm, cut these into 23 squares (Q) 2⅞ in/7.5 cm;

1 strip (R) 2½ in/6.5 cm;

1 square, 13 x 13 in/34 x 34 cm and cut in half on the diagonal (S).

● **Green fabric:** (diagram 3)

Cut off a 82 in/205 cm length and remove the selvages. Cutting parallel with the selvage, cut:

2 strips (1) 3½ in/9 cm;

2 strips (2) 1½ in/4 cm;

1 strip, 3½ in/9 cm, from this cut a length (3) 40½ in/101.5 cm; trim the remaining portion of this strip to 2½ in/6.5 cm wide, from this cut 1 piece (4) 26½ in/66.5 cm long, and 1 piece (5) 14½ in/36.5 cm;

1 strip, 2½ in/6.5 cm, from this cut a piece (6) 38½ in/96.5 cm; trim the remaining portion of this strip to 1½ in/4 cm wide, from this cut 1 strip (7) 39½ in/99 cm.

diagram 1

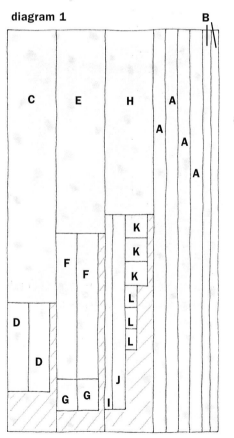

diagram 2

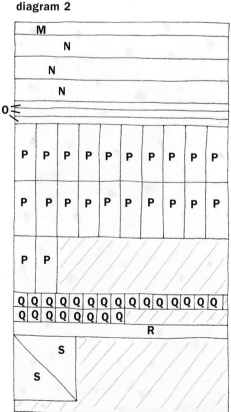

diagram 3   **diagram 4**

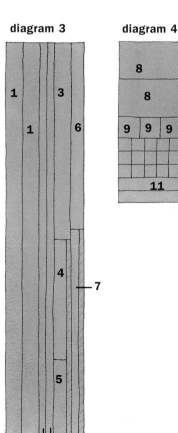

Cutting across the remaining width of the fabric (diagram 4), cut:

2 strips (8) 8½ in/21.5 cm;

1 strip 4⅞ in/12.5 cm, cut this into 3 squares (9) 4⅞ in/12.5 cm;

3 strips 2⅞ in/7.5 cm, cut these into 23 squares (10) 2⅞ in/7.5 cm;

2 strips (11) 2⅝ in/7 cm.

● **Blue flower fabric**, cut

6 strips, 2½ in/6.5 cm;

2 strips, 4½ in/11.5 cm.

● **Yellow fabric**, cut

1 strip, 1½ in/4 cm;

3 squares, 2½ in/6.5 cm.

STITCHING

1 Take one background square (Q) and one green square (10) and place right sides together. Using the quick piecing method of two triangles in a square, stitch together along the diagonal. Cut apart and press the seam towards the green fabric. Use all twenty-three squares of each fabric to make forty-six squares in total (diagram 5).

diagram 5

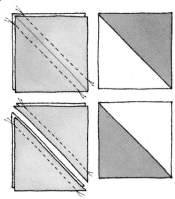

2 Take one background strip (O) and stitch a blue 2½ in/6.5 cm strip to either side of it. Press the seams towards the blue fabric. Repeat to make three units in total (diagram 6).

diagram 6

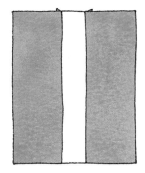

3 To all three units stitch one background strip N) to one side of the blue strips. Press the seam towards the blue fabric. Cross-cut these units into forty-six 2½ in/6.5 cm strips (diagram 7).

diagram 7

4 Stitch one of the squares made in step 1 to each of these strips, taking care to turn the square so that the green "leaves" will be pointing in the correct direction. Half the units will have the leaves facing left and half will be facing right (diagram 8).

diagram 8

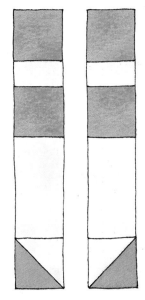

5 Stitch the 1½ in/4 cm yellow strip to one background strip (M). Press the seam towards the yellow fabric.

6 Stitch the long edge of the two green strips (8) to the yellow strip. Press the seam towards the yellow. Cross-cut into twenty-three 1½ in/4 cm strips (diagram 9).

diagram 9

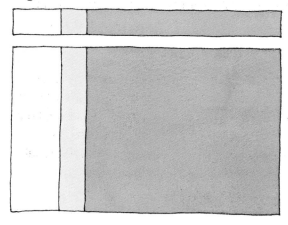

7 Stitch two of the units made in step 4 to either side of the unit just made. Take care to put the units in the correct position (diagram 10). Press the seams towards the stem. Make a total of 23 of these flower units.

diagram 10

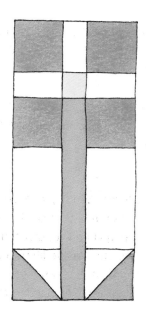

8 Stitch a background rectangle (P) to the righthand side of eighteen of the flowers.

9 Trim two of the remaining P-rectangles to measure 11½ x 3½ in/29 x 9 cm.

10 For the lefthand border, stitch eight of the units made in step 8 together. To the left of the first flower (the top edge of the quilt), stitch one of the trimmed P-rectangles. To the other end of the border, stitch one flower unit without a P-rectangle. Trim one of the background strips (B) to the correct length, 80½ in/201.5 cm, and stitch it to

this border above the flowers. Trim a strip of green fabric (1) to the correct length, 80½ in/ 201.5 cm, and stitch it to this border below the flowers (diagram 11).

11 For the righthand border, stitch eight flower units created in step 8 together. Stitch another flower unit without a P-rectangle to the righthand end of this border unit and to that stitch the remaining trimmed P-rectangle. After joining all the flower units together, stitch the two border strips into place as described in step 10 (diagram 12).

diagram 11   **diagram 12**

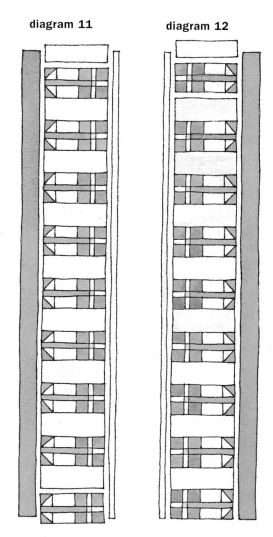

12 Trim ¼ in/0.75cm off the 11½ in/29 cm edge of the two remaining background rectangles (P). This is necessary to make the flowers fit across the bottom. Stitch these trimmed rectangles to either side of one of the remaining flower units. This will be the centre flower in the group of five that make up the border for the bottom edge of the quilt. Stitch the remaining flower units together to form the border as illustrated. Stitch the background strip (I) and the green strip (3) above and below the group of five flowers (diagram 13).

diagram 13

13 Stitch a green strip (11) to the long edge of each of the two corner triangles (S). Stitch one bordered corner triangle to the right end of the lefthand border and one to the left end of the righthand border (diagram 14).

diagram 14

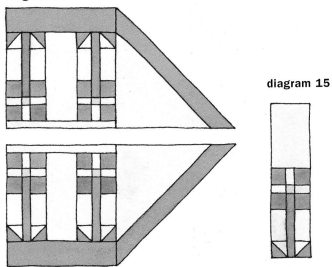

diagram 15

14 Using the squares of background fabric (K) and the green fabric squares (9), stitch together to create the two triangles in a square unit as in step 1.

15 Stitch a 4½ in/11.5 cm blue strip to either side of background strip (M). Press the seams towards the blue fabric. Cross-cut into six 4½ in/11.5 cm segments.

16 To make the short centre flower, stitch a 2½ in/6.5 cm yellow square to one end of a green strip (5). To the end with the yellow square, stitch a piece of background fabric (L). Stitch a piece of background fabric (G) to two of the flower petal units made in step 15. To the background fabric on each of these units stitch one of the leaf units made in step 14, ensuring that the leaves are facing the correct direction. Assemble the complete flower unit as for the border flowers (diagram 10). Stitch background fabric strip (C) to the top (diagram 15).

17 To make the middle centre flower, repeat step 16, but use the background fabric (D) and (E) and the green fabric (4).

18 To make the tall centre flower, repeat step 16, but use the background fabric (F) and (H) and the green fabric (6).

19 Following the quilt assembly diagram on page 132, trim two of the background strips (A) to 77½ in/194 cm. Stitch one between the short and middle flower and one between the middle and tall flower, positioning the flowers so that the short one is on the left and the tall one is on the right.

20 Stitch background fabric strip (J) to the bottom edge of the three flower unit.

21 Trim the remaining two strips of background fabric (A) to the correct measurement, 79½ in/199 cm, and stitch one on each side of the three flower unit.

22 Stitch the green strip (7) to the edge below the flowers and stitch the two green strips (2), one on either side of the unit.

23 Stitch the flower border with the five flowers to the lower edge of the quilt and stitch the appropriate side flower border to each side.

FINISHING

1 Sandwich the quilt top, wadding and backing for quilting and pin or baste together. Quilt in your chosen design. This quilt was quilted with diagonal lines across the background fabric and "in-the-ditch" around each of the flowers, their stems and leaves. There are five rows of quilting on the border running parallel with the edge.

2 Use the remaining fabric scraps to create 2½ in/6.5 cm bias binding strips. Join the strips together to create a single strip that is long enough to go all round the quilt. The binding on this quilt matches the areas of the quilt that it touches. You may, of course, choose to bind the quilt in one colour only.

Climbing Roses

The traditional Amish design of "Bars" is a much loved one, probably for its bold simplicity. Using a floral colour scheme with floral quilting motifs gives this quilt a fresh country flowers interpretation. The quilt is speedily made, having only nine pieces, plus the piping, thus allowing the busy modern quiltmaker time to relax and enjoy the quilting process. Big Stitch quilting using Perlé thread has been used for the more decorative portions of the quilting.

MATERIALS

All fabrics used in this quilt top are 45 in/115 cm wide, 100% cotton

Border, floral: 2½ yards/2.5 metres
White: 1 yard/1 metre
Piping, lavender: ¼ yard/25 cm
Backing: 51 x 63 in/130 x 160 cm
Wadding: 2 oz, 51 x 63 in/130 x 160 cm
Threads: Quilting thread to match; Perlé No. 8 in a contrasting colour

Quilt size: 47 x 59 in/120 x 150 cm

Quilt assembly diagram

CUTTING

- **Border, floral:** cut a piece 17 in/42.5 cm off the length of the fabric and retain for the binding; cutting parallel with the selvage: 2 pieces, 8½ x 60½ in/21.5 x 151.5 cm; 2 pieces, 8½ x 47½ in/21.5 x 119 cm; 2 pieces, 4½ x 43½ in/11.5 x 109 cm.
- **White:** 3 strips, 8½ x 43½ in/21.5 x 109 cm.
- **Piping, lavender:** 6 strips, ¾ x 43½ in/2 x 109 cm; 6 strips, ¾ x 8½ in/2 x 21.5 cm.

STITCHING

All seam allowances are the usual ¼ in/0.75 cm.

1 Fold the piping strips in half along the length with wrong sides together and press.

2 Place one 8½ in/21.5 cm folded piping strip along each short edge of the plain fabric strips, aligning all raw edges. Baste into position (diagram 1).

diagram 1   **diagram 2**

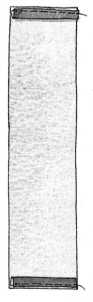
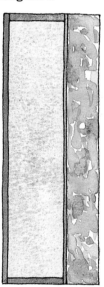

3 Place a 43½ in/109 cm folded piping strip along each long side of the plain strips, aligning all raw edges. Baste these into position.

4 Place a 4½ in/11.5 cm border fabric strip right sides together with one of the plain strips aligning all the raw edges. Stitch together down the long edge, taking care to keep the seam allowance even thus ensuring that the finished piping will be of a consistent width (diagram 2). Repeat this procedure with another plain strip and the second border fabric strip of the same length.

5 Now stitch the two units just completed together along their long edges, alternating the plain and border fabric strips. Add a third plain strip to the free border strip (diagram 3).

diagram 3

6 This five-strip unit will now measure 32½ x 43½ in/ 81.5 x 109 cm. At the corners place a mark on the wrong side ¼ in/0.75 cm in from each edge.

7 On the wrong sides of the remaining 8½ in/21.5 cm border strips, find the centre point. From this point, measure out in both directions, 16¼ in/40.75 cm for the top and bottom borders, and 22¼ in/54.5 cm for the side borders. Place a mark ¼ in/0.75 cm from the edge of the fabric at these measured points (diagram 4). These marks will correspond to those on the five-strip unit.

diagram 4

8 You may find it helpful to mark in a stitching line for the mitred corner at this stage. Place your rotary cutting ruler so that the 45 degree line falls along the edge of the fabric and the edge of the ruler on the mark that you made in the previous step. Draw a line along the edge of the ruler from the mark to the edge of the fabric, (diagram 5).

diagram 5

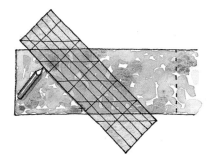

9 Place the appropriate border strip right sides together with the quilt top, aligning the raw edges and the marks made on the corners of the quilt unit and the border strip. Stitch the border strip to the quilt top, beginning and ending at the marks. Secure the stitching by back-stitching at these points. Stitch all four border strips into position (diagram 6).

diagram 6

10 Fold the quilt diagonally so that two border strips are right sides together and the mitre lines previously drawn are correctly aligned one on top of the other. Stitch along the mitre line beginning at the point where the stitching starts on the border strip and finishing where the stitching stops on the quilt top, remembering to secure the stitching at this point (diagram 7).

diagram 7

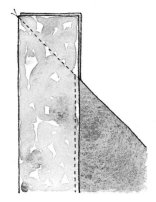

11 Open out the seam and examine it from the front. If all is well (the border lies flat, the stitched seam

reaches the junction of the border/quilt), trim the seam allowance to ¼ in/0.75 cm. Press this seam open and press the quilt/border seam towards the border. Repeat steps 10 and 11 on the three remaining corners (diagram 8).

diagram 8

FINISHING

1 Mark the quilting designs on the pieced top. Use the motif on page 142 for the plain panels, then mark a square-on-point grid with a ruler behind the roses. Mark the border motif from page 142 on the borders.

2 Spread the backing right side down on a flat surface, then smooth the wadding and the quilt top, right side up on top. Fasten with safety pins or baste in a grid.

3 Quilt the panel and border motifs using perlé no. 8 thread. Quilt the grid behind the roses using quilting thread, then stitch three rows of quilting on the fabric between the plain strips and two rows around the centre group of five strips.

4 Mark the curved "corners" on the quilt using your own curve. This mark will represent the edge of the quilt when applying the binding (diagram 9).

diagram 9

5 Make the bias binding 2½ in/6.5 cm wide using the continuous strip method and the remaining 17 in/ 42.5 cm piece of border fabric. Bind the edges with a double-fold binding, trimming the corners as necessary.

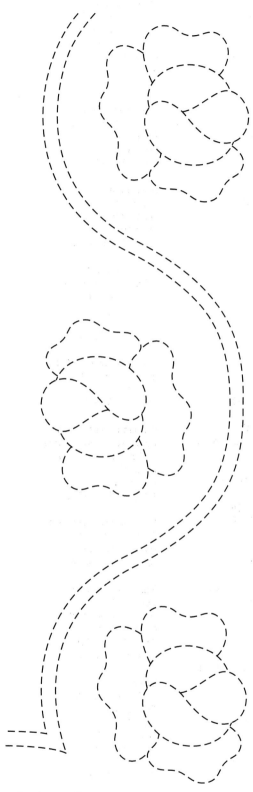

border motif

panel motif

SUPPLIERS

UK

The Colour Room
32 High Street
Mildenhall, Bury St. Edmunds
Suffolk IP28 7EA
Tel: 01638 716686
Needlecraft retailers and
longarm quilting services

The Cotton Patch
1285 Stratford Road
Hall Green
Birmingham B28 9AJ
Tel: 0121 702 2840
Patchwork and quilting supplies
Catalogue available

Creative Quilting
3 Bridge Road
East Molesey
Surrey KT8 9EU
Tel: 020 8941 7075
Specialist retailer

Custom Quilting Ltd
"Beal na Tra"
Derrymihan West
Castletownbere
Co. Cork, Ireland
Email: patches@iol.ie
Longarm quilting services

Fred Aldous Ltd
P.O. Box 135, 37 Lever Street
Manchester M1 1LW
Tel: 0161 236 2477
Mail order craft materials

Joseph's Coat
The Limes, Cowbridge
Vale of Glamorgan
Tel: 01446 775620
Patchwork and quilting supplies

Patchwork Direct
c/o Heirs & Graces
King Street, Bakewell
Derbyshire DE45 1DZ
Tel: 01629 815873
www.patchworkdirect.com
Patchwork and quilting supplies
and accessories

Piecemakers
13 Manor Green Road
Epsom, Surrey KT19 8RA
Tel: 01372 743161
Specialist retailer

Purely Patchwork
23 High Street
Linlithgow, Scotland
Tel: 01506 846200
Patchwork and quilting supplies

Stitch in Time
293 Sandycombe Road
Kew, Surrey TW9 3LU
Tel: 020 8948 8462
www.stitchintimeuk.com
Specialist quilting retailer

Strawberry Fayre
Chagford
Devon TQ13 8EN
Tel: 01647 433250
Mail order supplier of fabrics
and quilting supplies

Sunflower Fabrics
157-159 Castle Road
Bedford MK40 3RS
Tel: 01234 273819
www.sunflowerfabrics.com
Quilting supplies

The Quilt Loft
9/10 Havercroft Buildings
North Street
Worthing
West Sussex BN11 1DY
Tel: 01903 233771
Quilt supplies, classes
and workshops

The Quilt Room
20 West Street
Dorking
Surrey RH4 1BL
Tel: 01306 740739
www.quiltroom.co.uk
Mail order:
The Quilt Room
c/o Carvilles
Station Road
Dorking
Surrey RH4 1XH
Tel: 01306 877307
Specialist retailer

South Africa

Stitch 'n' Stuff
140 Lansdowne Road
Claremont 7700
Tel: 021 674 4059

Pied Piper
69 1st Avenue
Port Elizabeth 6001
Tel: 041 365 1616

Quilt Talk
40 Victoria Street
George 6530
Tel: 044 873 2947

Nimble Fingers
Shop 222, Village Mall
Village Road
Kloof 3610
Tel: 031 764 628

Quilt Tech
9 Louanna Avenue
Kloofendal
Extension 5 1709
Tel: 011 679 4386

Simply Stitches
2 Topaz Street
Albernarle
Germiston 1401
Tel: 011 902 6997

Quilting Supplies
42 Nellnapius Drive
Irene 0062
Tel: 012 667 2223

Australia

Patchwork Plus
15 Jackson Avenue
Miranda
NSW 2228
Tel: (02) 9540 2786

Patchwork Addiction
96 Fletcher Street
Essendon
VIC 3040
Tel: (03) 9372 0793

Quilts and Threads
827 Lower North East Road
Dernancourt
SA 5075
Tel: (08) 8365 6711

Riverlea Cottage Quilts
Shop 9, 330 Unley Road
Hyde Park
SA 5061
Tel: (08) 8373 0653

Country Patchwork Cottage
10/86 Erindale Road
Balcatta
WA 6021
Tel: (08) 9345 3550

Country Patchwork Cottage
5/3 South Street
Canning Vale
WA 6155
Tel: (08) 9455 2815

Patchwork Supplies
43 Gloucester Street
Highgate Hill
QLD 4101
Tel: (07) 3844 9391

The Quilters Store
22 Shaw Street
Auchenflower
QLD 4066
Tel: (07) 3870 0408

New Zealand

Patches of Ponsonby
2A Kelmarna Avenue
Herne Bay
Auckland
Tel: (09) 376 1556

Patchwork Barn
132 Hinemoa Street
Birkenhead
Auckland
Tel: (09) 480 5401

Daydreams
P.O. Box 69072
Glendene
Auckland
Tel: (09) 837 0019

Stitch and Craft
32 East Tamaki Road
Hunter's Corner
Auckland
Tel: (09) 278 1351
Fax: (09) 278 1356

The Patchwork Shop
356 Grey Street
Hamilton
Tel: (07) 856 6365

**Grandmothers Garden
Patchwork and Quilting**
1042 Gordonton Road
Gordonton
Hamilton
Tel: (07) 824 3050

Needlecraft Distributors
600 Main Street
Palmerston North
Tel: (06) 356 4793

**Hands Ashford Craft
Supply Store**
5 Normands Road
Christchurch
Tel: (03) 355 9099
www.hands.co.nz

Stitches
351 Colombo Street
Christchurch
Tel: (03) 379 1868
Fax: (03) 377 2347
www.stitches.co.nz

Patchwork Plus
608 Colombo Street
Christchurch
Tel: (03) 366 9315

Variety Handcrafts
106 Princes Street
Dunedin
Tel: (03) 474 1088

INDEX

Acknowledgements

The publishers would like to thank
Tissu Créatif for supplying the
fabrics for "Red Sky At Night"
and "Rain Before Seven".

Tissu Créatif
European Fabric Specialists
Brittany France
Mail order Dept. (only)
La Basse Landrie
22100 Trevron
FRANCE